ETHICS IN GOVERNANCE

RESOLUTION OF DILEMMAS

With Case Studies

Second Edition

Mohan Kanda

CENTRE FOR GOOD GOVERNANCE
Knowledge • Technology • People

BSP **BS Publications**
A unit of **BSP Books Pvt. Ltd.**

ETHICS IN GOVERNANCE
Resolution of Dilemmas
With Case Studies, Second Edition

Cover design by: Anantha Laxmi Juvvadi

Published by BS Publications in association with "Centre for Good Governance, Hyderabad"

Published by

CENTRE FOR GOOD GOVERNANCE
Knowledge • Technology • People

(Dr. MCR HRD Institute Campus),
Road No. 25, Jubilee Hills, Hyderabad 500033
Telangana (India)
www.cgg.gov.in
Phone: +91 40 2354 1907 / 09
Fax: +91 40 2354 1953
Email: info@cgg.gov.in

BSP **BS Publications**
A unit of **BSP Books Pvt. Ltd.**

4-4-309/316, Giriraj Lane, Sultan Bazar,
Hyderabad - 500 095
Phone : 040 - 23445605, 23445688
e-mail : info@bspbooks.net

ISBN: 978-93-85433-68-9 (HB)

For

my father

the Late **Sri Justice Kanda Bhimasankaram**

who introduced me to the joys of reading
and, more importantly, taught me what lay beyond.

I have, on occasion, managed to imitate him.
I realized long ago that it is impossible to emulate him.

V.S SAMPATH
Chief Election Commissioner of India

सत्यमेव जयते

भारत निर्वाचन आयोग
Election Commission of India

Foreword

Ethics is gaining prominence in the debates on Governance in recent years on account of increasing expectations from people in regard to ethical standards in public services. There is a general perception across the country that values and standards in the delivery of public services are on the decline. This raises questions about the costs of misconduct on the part of public servants, costs in terms of losses in trust and confidence in public institutions charged with promoting economic and social development. There is a move worldwide to restore a measure of trust in the integrity of public institutions and officials, to improve the quality of service delivery and promote better governance. It can be argued that the perception of a fall in public standards in linked to the shifting role of the State, which is going through a rapid process of reform, liberalization, privatization and globalization along with advances in technology and aspirations of people.

Public service as on institution is under pressure to transform itself to respond to these challenges. As public servants are asked to take on new and sometimes conflicting roles, need is being increasingly felt for a cost-effective structure and an enabling environment to bring about desirable standards in conduct and behaviour.

Ethics can be defined as a set of standards that society places on itself which helps guide behaviour, choices and actions. Persons involved in the delivering of public services face ethical dilemmas in the discharge of their functions, their behaviour towards colleagues and in dealing with issues arising in interaction with other stakeholders.

An attempt is made in this work to deal with origins of ethics, evolution of great ethical traditions, theories of how one ought to behave and arguments about specific ethical issues. The book provides critical information and refers to the personal experiences of a senior public servant in the fields of ethics and integrity in governance, along with emerging perspectives. It addresses the key dimensions of values in public service, of governance and maintenance of ethical standards.

Institutions and laws depend on the individuals who operate them. Public servants have the responsibility to ensure that the services provided are not only effective, efficient and reliable, but also that their delivery is free from corruption and malpractices. This applies not only to public officials but also to political leaders, elected, or appointed.

I am particularly delighted at the opportunity of offering foreword for on eminently useful book by a distinguished senior colleague of mine Dr. Mohan Kanda with whom I had the privilege of working for decades together. The book in every aspect bears the mark of rich, practical and conceptual experience of the Author.

I hope the book will serve not only as a guiding spirit for public servants but also prove of interest to other readers with its wide gamut of subjects and case studies covered.

V. S. Sampath

(V.S. Sampath)

April 2014
New Delhi

Nirvachan Sadan, Ashoka Road, New Delhi 110001, Tel : (O) 23716552, 23713689 Fax : 23711023
Email: vs.sampath@eci.gov.in Website: www.eci.nic.in

Messages to Second Edition

I congratulate Dr. Mohan Kanda for authoring a book on a subject of vital importance in today's world. "Ethics in Governance- Resolution of dilemmas with Case studies" is a relevant book for civil services aspirants and serving officers. Governance is not about rowing the ship like the stewardship that guides the direction of the ship. Further, Governance is about setting and deciding the direction of an organization and how one influences it.

Dr. Kanda's competence lies in the ethics and values he believes in. He has always believed in the three E's -excel, exceed and expand. His forte is the ability to take his team along with him. Dr.Kanda has structured the book in a way which follows the ABCs of any great book- accuracy, brevity and clarity. These qualities are the cornerstones of this book. The lucid way in which the book has been written makes it a fantastic read. The book fills gap in the reading material available in the market - with theories as well as the dilemmas faced by public servants and how they can be resolved. It provides case studies along with recommended approaches that will help the readers in making decisions when one is at the crossroads of seemingly close choices. My complements are to Dr.Kanda for keeping the logos, pathos and ethos intact in the book. I feel confident that more editions will come out in the future.

M. Gopalakrishna, IAS (Retd)

Formerly Chairman, Rural Electrification Corporation,

Government of India

"I was delighted to read Mohan Kanda's book 'Ethics in Governance'. His delineation of the concept of ethics in all its dimensions, relating that to the concept of governance in general and governance in India, in particular, is appreciative. Einstein had differentiated a successful person from a purposeful person; the former being one who takes the maximum from the society and giving the least to it and the latter taking the least from the society and giving the maximum to it. Mohan's message is that ethics will generate purposeful persons rather than successful persons.

The road map suggested by Mohan is a good first step, which will march India towards governance informed by ethics. I suggest Mohan should carry forward his message strongly to sub serve and achieve the title of his book."

Dr. S. Chakravarthy, IAS (Retd)

Formerly Spl. Chief Secretary to Government of A.P.
and Member, MRTP Commission

Messages to First Edition

"This book is a rich source of thought on the subject 'Ethics in Governance.' It forms a valuable compendium to all the people who are in public service now or aspiring to come into civil service in future, as it contains the perceptions, experiences and experiments of a conscientious civil servant. As such, all the public servants whoever wish to retire from service with a clean conscience, the richest treasure a man can have, would do well to study the book at least once".

Swami Jnanadananda
Adhyaksha, Ramakrishna Math, Hyderabad.

"Ever since it has been noticed that the Union Public Service Commission has been conducting All India Services Examinations like IAS without any prior knowledge about the role of Ethics in the Government, there has been a clamour from several experts for making the examination's a broad based test. Hence the UPSC introduced recently preliminary test like Ethics in Governance which has assumed lot of importance in recent times.

"Ethics in Governance- Resolution of Dilemmas, with case studies" by Dr. Mohan Kanda provides a holistic perspectivii)ve on the much talked topic of Ethics and Governance.

The real life incidents narrated by Dr. Kanda provides important insights into situations that one may face while holding public office. His experience will definitely provide valuable guidance to public servants, as well as Civil Service aspirants".

P. Abraham, IAS (Retd)
Formerly, Member, Union Public Service Commission of India.
Secretary, Ministry of Power, Government of India.

"The symbiotic relationship between good governance, integrity, ethical conduct and universal values has been acknowledged since times immemorial. However, it has come into prominence in a big way in recent times, the world over, particularly in the context of public policy making and delivery of public goods and services. Dr. Mohan Kanda's magnum opus has, therefore, come at an opportune time when the country finds itself in the midst of an unprecedented politico-administrative churning. It explores a vast gamut of ethical principles and practices that the civil servants of today have to bear in mind at all times. Practical wisdom to deal with ethical and moral dilemmas faced by the bureaucracy has been presented precisely and succinctly through a wide range of case studies. A must read for all aspirants as well as new entrants to the esteemed portals of civil services".

Vivek K. Agnihotri, IAS (Retd.)
Former Secretary-General, Rajya Sabha

"It is a very refreshing and timely book, written by someone who has practiced ethics and Dharma all his life in his career of more than three decades of governance. The lessons from various case studies so convincingly bring out the dilemmas faced by practitioners in different situations and how then to determine the righteous path? Even Arjuna faced these questions when he turned towards Lord Krishna for guidance. But while challenges as well as perception of what is right and what is wrong may vary in different ages, the basic tenets of ethics and Kartavya for larger public good ever remain the same. This publication will undoubtedly serve a big need at this juncture when the governance is the focus of national debate".

Dhanendra Kumar, IAS (Retd.)
Former Chair Person
Competition Commission of India.

Preface to Second Edition

Ethics and Governance have interested me ever since I started my journey in public service more than four decades ago. In this work I have refrained from dealing with theory as much as possible and have, instead relied on earthly wisdom and real life incidents. This has been done to highlight the difference between theory, concepts and their practice.

Ethics as the overarching framework for the application of acceptable principles is an important concern today. The case studies dealt with herein will hopefully prove useful in understanding and responding to the demands of the day to day situations.

Ethics and compliance go together in the governance milieu of the public as well as corporate sectors. The importance of strategic leadership of ethical behaviour in their activities can no longer be ignored.

This book will have more than served its purpose if its contents can at least in part inform the initiation of such a process in the future. I am happy that this book provided me with an opportunity to share with the readers the experiences I had during my career and the lessons I learnt.

I hope this book will provide useful insights to students preparing for the civil services examinations, as also for those in public service. It is gratifying that the book has proved worthy of a reprint.

Mohan Kanda

Acknowledgements

So many people have contributed so much to the making of this book that I can hardly do justice to the task of expressing my gratitude to all of them.

My thanks are due, in particular, to Sri K. Ramakrishna Rao, IAS, Director General, Centre for Good Governance, Hyderabad for accepting the idea of a book and offering to support its publication.

I wish to thank the management, the staff and the students of the Sri Chaitanya IAS Academy, the lectures which I gave there being the source of inspiration for this effort.

I am grateful to Dr. S.K. Rao, Director General, Administrative Staff College of India (ASCI) for encouraging me to write this book.

I sincerely thank Sri Devi Prasad Juvvadi, Director (Agriculture Management) of the Centre for Good Governance and his team comprising Sarvasri Kiran Kumar, Mayank Kashyap, Raja Panchal, Kumari Sumana Chatterjee for the extraordinary assiduity and care that they have put into editing of the contents of this book. I also thank Smt. Anantha Laxmi Juvvadi for designing the cover page and Sri Avinash Venkata Adavikolanu for his assistance during the second edition.

I wish to place on record my sincere appreciation of the assistance readily extended by Sri P.V.A. Rama Rao, formerly Managing Director, NABARD.

Such refinement as the contents of this book have undergone is due to the patient scrutiny they were subjected to by my daughter and sparring partner Smt. Aparna Kanda who is still struggling to appreciate the difference between frankness and bluntness!

Hopefully her input will have added a contemporary touch to the effort. But for her uncanny knack to spot weaknesses and suggest appropriate changes, the book would have had many more short comings than it might now have.

I wish to record my gratitude to Sri C. Sriram who did an excellent job going through the book with customary diligence and offered many valuable comments.

This book would not have been possible but for the hard work and application of my colleague Sri K.V. Ramakrishna Rao.

Mohan Kanda
Hyderabad, 18th December 2015

Contents

1. ETHICS

Ethics is a code of integrated values which guides our actions and choices and determines the purpose and course of our lives. It is simply a principle that helps promote, enhance, and maintain our lives. Each individual has an influence on society considering that all people and things around them are affected by their choices whether they be good or bad, In that sense ethics play a very important role in our lives. It influences the choices of individuals and eventually determines who they become. Our interpretation of what is wrong and right and how we act upon these interpretations helps us in forming our beliefs, standards, and personalities.

1.1 Introduction

"Ethics is knowing the difference between what you have a right to do and what is right to do".

- Potter Stewart

Ethics as a term in philosophy has several meanings which are open to interpretation, with the meaning often contested. For some authors it is about the *absence* of something such as misconduct or fraud, while others describe it as *presence* of personal and professional values such as honesty, integrity etc. But we need to seek a basic understanding of what it is actually understood as.

The term ethics comes from the Greek word *ethos,* which means "character". Many conceptions of ethics in the ancient world were highly influenced by the Greeks, particularly Aristotle and Plato. According to Plato people naturally desire happiness but the problem lies in identifying how to bring it about. And, if in conquest of happiness they do something wrong which is unintentional, the ethical difficulties arising in this situation could be *epistemological* in nature. Plato suggested four virtues namely wisdom, temperance, justice and courage that define ethics.

Aristotle, went further and described in his *Nicomachean Ethics*, that an act is good because the person doing it is good and it is not the act which is good by itself. In other words something virtuous is good because it is done aiming for the best.

In philosophy, ethics studies the moral behaviour of humans and defines as to how one should act. Ethics is concerned with right or wrong behavior when faced with moral choices. It seeks to resolve questions dealing with human morality—concepts such as good and evil, right and wrong, virtue and vice, justice and crime. It is about systematizing, defending, and recommending the concepts of what could be construed as right and wrong behaviour.

According to James Fieser, Professor of Philosophy at the University of Tennessee at Martin, ethics may be divided into four major areas of study:

(i) **Meta-ethics** is concerned with the theoretical meaning and reference of moral propositions and how their truth values (if any) may be determined;

(ii) **Normative ethics,** deals with the practical means of determining a moral course of action;

(iii) **Applied ethics,** studies how moral outcomes can be achieved in specific situations;

(iv) **Descriptive ethics,** (also known as comparative ethics) is the study of people's beliefs about morality;

Meta-ethics investigates where our ethical principles come from, and what they mean. The term comes from "meta" which means '*after or beyond*' which can be interpreted as the bird's eye view of entire ethical concepts. Meta-ethics covers two prominent issues which are (a) *metaphysical* issues concerning the existence of morality sans humans and (b) *psychological* issues concerning the underlying basis of our conduct and moral judgments.

Normative ethics examines the morality of actions whether they are right or wrong. It can also be described as a test of one's own behaviour. Confucius's 'Golden Rule' is a perfect example of normative principle, "Do not do to others what you do not want to be done to yourself" or as the Bible says "Do unto others as you would have them do to you". For instance, I would not like somebody to lie to me and it would be morally wrong for me to lie to someone else. The key assumption here is about having only one criterion of moral conduct.

Applied ethics deals with the analysis of very specific, controversial and debatable moral issues such as euthanasia, LGBT rights and the right to abortion etc. These issues for the sake of convenience, have been divided into groups such as medical ethics, business ethics, sexual ethics and environmental ethics etc. For an issue to be categorized as one of the applied ethical concerns there must be a significant number of people both for and against it. The issue of fake encounters by the police would not be applied ethics since majority of the people agree that it is wrong. By contrast, the issue of same sex marriages would qualify as applied ethics issue since there are large groups of people both for and against it.

Descriptive ethics in simple words is a comparative ethics which studies people's beliefs about morality. It investigates how ideals, actions and morals are condemned or accepted in different societies at different times. Every generation may have different set of morals and ideals which they consider ethics. Descriptive ethics oversee whether the same set of ethics holds true for different generations and the changes they have undergone in subsequent generations. Lawrence Kohlberg, a psychologist who worked extensively on Descriptive ethics conducted an experiment by questioning a group of boys about a person facing a moral dilemma: Should a person steal lifesaving drugs to save his wife or refrain from the theft even though it would lead to her death?

Kohlberg was less concerned about the choices the boys made than in the reasoning they gave to support their answers. The choice they made was directly related to the set of ethics they believed in. Descriptive ethics describes moral development of human beings though the empirical lens.

The following questions would perhaps highlight the difference between the above mentioned fields of ethics:

- **Meta-ethics:** What does 'right' mean?
- **Normative (prescriptive) ethics:** How should people act?
- **Applied ethics:** How does one imbibe moral knowledge and put it into practice?
- **Descriptive ethics:** What is right according to people?

Briefly speaking, ethics seeks to resolve various questions arising from human morality, concepts such as good and evil, right and wrong, virtue and vice, justice and crime. As Valdemar W. Setzer puts it "Ethics is not definable, is not implemental, because it is not conscious; it involves not only our thinking, but also our feeling. Not only do we need to know what ethics are, but we also need to want to act upon them". People can have the knowledge of right from wrong, but still have no desire to live and act in an ethical manner.

1.2 Dimensions of Ethics

Ethics as mentioned earlier refers to standards of right and wrong that prescribe what humans ought to do usually in terms of duties, principles, specific virtues or benefit to society. Ethical dimensions bring the study and exploration of ethics to life, and establish who one is and what one stands for.

Ethical dimensions concerned with the availability of choices and potential of some choices to impact negatively on others and those characterizing day to day work place activities can be both easy and difficult to identify. To assess the ethics of any action, it is useful to separate the three dimensions of action namely Prudence, Legality and Ethics.

Prudence: Prudence is the ability to discipline oneself by the use of reason. This dimension helps decide whether a given action is prudent or not. The action in question should be distinguished separately as prudent or otherwise. "Prudential judgment" is exercised when the circumstances must be weighed to determine the correct action. Generally, it applies to situations where two people could weigh the circumstances differently and come to different ethical conclusions. Prudence is defined within the Code of Governance as care, caution and good judgment as well as wisdom in looking ahead.

Legal: The rule of law is the core of democracy, and equality before the law is primary characteristic. Every action raises the question of legal dimension thereof which pertains to the law of the land, which in turn has a coercive aspect and includes obligations. Administrators have to respect the legal frame work. The administration works within the realm of law, it automatically sets forth for itself a series of controls and regulations. Governments and administrators have to work within the legal frame work.

Ethics: Society as a whole decides what ethical practice is in response to changing social values and the code of ethics of an organization determines its credibility. An action raises questions in the ethical dimension when it pertains to our pre-determined standards of right behaviour. An action in accord with the reflected code of behaviour is obviously ethical and in conflict unethical. Administrators need to distinguish the three dimensions of action and avoid confusion and complications in making decisions. One common mistake is to characterize emotionally charged prudential actions as ethically sensitive. Prudential elements can and do require balancing of various factors. It is while drawing the distinction between prudent, legal and ethical dimensions of actions, ethical dilemmas are encountered. Public servants need to respect the rights of citizens and serve the interests of society by following the principles and values of ethical governance.

1.3 Human Values

"In the world of values, nature in itself is neutral; it is we who create value and our desires which confer value... It is for us to determine the good life, not for nature - not even for nature personified as God."

- Bertrand Russell

Globalization and latest information technologies have posed many challenges to the society all over the world and India is no exception. One of the important areas that draws the attention of the society and individual thinkers is the deteriorating human value system. The focus is on how best we can integrate the globalization with our value system? Concern for the value system is increasing as a result of crisis of values in the society. Human values are closely integrated with human life and every human being lives by certain values. Human values are habit of thoughts.

The values that we as human beings develop indirectly by using our amazing brains to reason about behaviour are called as conceived values. And these values are foremost devices for dealing with all social interactions. Every human being is born neutral and like a clean slate, but one can attain or acquire certain values depending on the nurturing of the parents, teachers, circumstances, environment and geographical location. Scientific analysis of the natural origin of human values and understanding of the human nature can be obtained from the combined perspective of biology and social sciences. A value appears to be a norm which helps to differentiate between right and wrong. But the values are rooted in the very condition of human existence, hence our knowledge of these conditions that is of the human situation leads us to establishing values which have objective validity. The validity exists with regard to the existing man, outside of him there are no values. Value development is a continuous cumulative independent process influencing the personality development of individuals. Indian society with heterogeneous population belonging to diversified cultures, religions, creed requires a sustaining value system to strengthen the ethical functioning of the governance apparatus.

The inculcation of human values begins with the birth of an individual and continues till the end. Some of the major values have appealing commonality all over the world irrespective of religions and cultures and acquire universal relevance. According to Sir Isaiah Berlin, a Russian born British political theorist "... universal values ... are values that a great many human beings in the vast majority of places and situations, at almost all times, do in fact hold in common, whether consciously and explicitly or as expressed in their behaviour...". The commonly accepted basic five core human values are: *Truth, Love and care, Peace, Justice and Nonviolence.*

Truth: The truth in any context does not depend upon the will or wish of the individual. It is independent of desires, their related interests and opinions and has both individual and communal aspects as it is an inherent value in the human psyche. It is why no one likes to be called a liar. Further, it is much harder to sustain a lie than to maintain the truth, because one lie leads to another until the complexity is unmanageable. The Satya Sai teachings on Truth say *"Truth is that which is not modified by time, space or guna (attribute). It is the same forever, unaffected and unchanging; it is never proved false by some subsequent event or knowledge"*. The Upanishads preached it as the highest human value.

Love and Care: Love is universal, and, perhaps, the most important element in our lives and our relationships. Love is the root of global values of compassion, peace, integrity, respect and responsibility. It may be expressed in different ways such as parental love, patriotic love, and love in marriage, love for nature, the environment and forms of life such as birds and animals. Dedication and devotion are a variant expression of love.

Peace: The desire for peace and harmony and the disapproval of violence and terror are essential components for the quest of happiness. Peace among nations and cordial relationships between countries has been realised by the international organizations such as the UN.

Justice: The concept of justice is based on empathy and respect. Justice means what is good, what is right. And what is righteous in relation to others. It arises from an understanding of basic human equality and of right and wrong in the sharing or the distribution of food, material values, wealth and prosperity. Justice is also about human equality for reward, punishment or inconveniences, or suffering; or about price settings, payments, salaries etc. Our standard of justice about the sharing of values, like knowledge, education and opportunities for development etc., is a universal and basic virtue that has evolved through passage of time and in response to the changing imperatives of the extended environment.

Ethics and Justice go hand in hand and all ethics cannot be codified into laws, rules and regulations. The principles of natural justice enshrined in the Vedic culture and respected over time merit universal application.

- One should not be one's own judge
- None ought to be judged without being given an opportunity to be heard
- One should not only do justice but also be seen to be doing justice

Respect for local/contemporary customs and traditions is another tenet of ethics that has withstood the test of time. These unwritten values also need to inform every action.

1.4 Emotional Intelligence

Emotional intelligence (EI) is concerned with ability to recognize and manage emotions in oneself and in others. Although EI as a concept only took formal shape quite recently, the ideas behind it have been in vogue since the time of Mary Parker Follett - most importantly in the context of identifying the feelings that promote loyalty commitment to organizations, and improve the quality of performance. Display of high EI often creates an enabling environment and enhances the ethical outcomes within an organization. EI is playing an increasingly key role in governance. This is especially significant given that the response to various government processes and products depends crucially on the perceptions of the general public.

There is bountiful literature extolling the virtues of leadership but what is important here is the linkage to EI. The traditional view of the role of emotion in public leadership has emphasized the values of impersonality and dehumanization, as expounded by Max Weber. EI is crucial for the management of work relationships across various levels of employees. It impacts on the way public servants deal with people including peers, superior officers, stakeholders and citizens with whom they interact on a daily basis. Another reason why public servants need to be effective in managing relationships is the need to ensure legitimacy of their actions and establish their credibility. EI also helps make public servants accountable for their actions and is, thus, an integral part of the role of public leadership, in the ethical discharge of duties.

Ethical dilemmas and EI are often intertwined because leaders, particularly those in the management of public institutions, are expected to perceive and manage their own emotions and those of others - in order to make the best ethical decisions possible and to cope with the associated challenges.

Proper management of emotions, positive as well as negative, is an important aspect of management.

Good governance in the public sector has a major contribution to make to the development of the country and ethics constitutes the fulcrum of that effort. In the conduct of dealings ethically and morally, in containing the abuse of power and authority vested in public servants, and ensuring the discharge of duties in a manner informed by a firm commitment to the imperative of integrity, El plays central role.

EI is leads to employees being more satisfied with their work ethic, while helping them remain committed and emotionally attached to the organization they are part of. EI helps divert attention away from personal gain. Public servants high on EI can understand and manage their own emotions better and challenge the status quo prevalent in the organizations. EI has been found to enable advocacy for equality at the workplace, encourage employees to confront unjust treatment and deal effectively with hard- to- please superiors.

People with higher emotional intelligence generally perform better as a result of an increased ability to effectively deal with stressful situations and tough customers.

1.5 Ethics in Administration

"The whole art of Government consists in the art of being honest"

- Thomas Jefferson

The subject of ethics has for long been a controversial area of study in the professions of law, politics and public administration. The need to ensure that civil servants or career staff in government function within the regimes of legal and organizational controls led to the evolution of code/manuals and job descriptions defining the limits of their responsibilities. Administrators and bureaucrats cannot avoid making decisions, and in doing so they should attempt to make ethical decisions. Administrators have discretionary powers that go beyond the manuals, orders, job descriptions and legal framework of their position and duties, and professional ethics come in as guidelines.

The exercise of discretion by public servants affects people's lives in a direct, lasting, and sometimes in profound manner. Administrators thus need a broad and solid understanding of ethical theories and traditions, and methods for emphasizing the ethical dimensions of their conduct. Ethics in public administration is not a transient concept but an approach which has shown a great deal of sustainability, fundamental to the area of public administration. The ethical frame work identifies the general core values which should be recognized universally. These core values include the rule of law, impartiality, objectivity, transparency, accountability, professionalism, reliability and courtesy. The member states of European Union have for instance initiated measures to put in place an ethical frame work. The success of public governance depends on the conduct of public functionaries who are supposed to act fairly and impartially in their dealings with society and people.

Determinants of Ethics in public Administration: The purpose of public service is to essentially fulfill citizens' basic requirements and the promotion of privatization concept has placed a great demand for quality deliverance. Public civil servants are responsible and accountable for the provision of public services. The individual attributes of the administrator play a key role in decision making skills.

The major determinants of ethics factor in the public administration are generally accepted as:

Professional codes of conduct: A professional code of conduct helps maintain standards for individuals practising the profession in regard to accountability and responsibility. Codes of conduct are designed to anticipate and prevent certain types of unacceptable conduct for e.g., conflict of interest, misuse of information and illegal gratification. Most codes focus on "don'ts' rather than affirmative obligations. Sometimes these codes have been used as building blocks for the edifice of public administration. Countries such as Slovakia focused on ethics standards as a way to reengineer their entire public service system. A written code of conduct is necessary but never sufficient. A mechanism for enforcement and evaluation is essential preferably of self evaluating nature. Good codes need to be simple and easily understood; Hong Kong's independent commission against corruption is a model in this aspect.

Organizational structure with clear accountability: Organizations in this context include Government organizations which are managed by policies, guidelines and systems. And these instruments are to be subjected to reviews from time to time to tone up the efficiency of the public organizations. Accountability in the public organizations has become an increasingly complex issue for contemporary governance. Several changes in policies and public administration influence the complexion of accountability. The individual public servant is expected to remain responsible to his or her own conceptions of the law being administered, as well as for a set of internalized values.

The political organizational culture: A country's concept of public administration reflects its underlying philosophy in regard to the role of Society and the State. The term political culture was first used by the American Political Scientist, Gabriel Almond, in "Comparative Political System". In the words of Almond and Powell; "culture is the pattern of individual attitudes and orientations towards politics among the members of a political system". Lucian Pye, the renowned American Political Scientist and China scholar, writes that "political culture is the set of attitudes, beliefs and sentiments that give orders and meaning to a political process and that provide the underlying assumptions and rules that govern behaviour in the political system. It encompasses both the political ideals and the operating norms of a polity. Political culture is thus the manifestation in aggregate form of the psychological and subjective dimensions of politics". Politics will always be a part of organizations so long as people are involved. Organizations that are overrun by politics, however, will sooner or later take their place among the ranks. Political decisions encourage hypocrisy, secrecy, deal making, rumors, power brokers, self-interests, image building, self-promotion, and cliques - not a recipe for effective teamwork. The process of ethics obviously depends on true political will.

Organizational Culture

The organizational culture comprises attitudes, experiences, beliefs and values of an organization and also defines the ethical climate. Ethical climate in an organization enables normative understanding of the issues at hand. It influences the policy making at various levels. For instance, ethical decisions could range from strategic issues such as levels of performance to day to day operational concerns as the giving or receiving of gifts.

This is also expected to play out in the way accountability roles are defined, and the degree to which organizations are autonomous and free from influence.

Management ethics involves dealings with different stakeholders, each of whom demands a separate set of requirements. The inherent ethical culture that resides in the organization plays a vital part in promoting a dialogue amongst the stakeholders on all aspects concerning ethics and helps advance the awareness that is already built in. Thus the culture of ethics pervades through from the leadership at the helm to across all levels and across all functions/ departments in the organization. This has several positive implications on multiple levels. It has been shown for instance, that such organizations perform better and are also sustainable in the long run - as relationships with investors, partners and employers are likely to be managed more effectively. Such a culture also helps in the decision making process that is inherent in the organization because strategic decisions taken by the leadership have a deep and wide impact on all the stakeholders concerned. As a result of organizational actions, confidence is built among the different stakeholders concerned well defined. Frameworks and mechanisms significantly aid the roles of regulatory agencies which involve constant monitoring of the impact of their actions.

1.6 Public Service and Dilemmas

A dilemma has wider dimensions than an ordinary problem and demands considered response. An ethical dilemma arises from a situation that necessitates a choice between competing sets of principles. Confrontations with the fundamental question what to do and how to act in complex situations and to the extent that present contrast in values causes the emergence of such an ethical dilemma. The decision maker may face unwelcome alternatives which may be mutually exclusive in the sense that one can only be chosen if the other is sacrificed. Conflicts of interests are the most obvious example that could place the public administrators in a dilemma and cause confusion and embarrassment. Awareness of the ethical dimensions and their code of conduct can help politicians and public servants follow socially accepted norms of behaviour. Difficult ethical dimensions may arise in the relationship between the personal and public life of politicians and public servants. Most ethical dilemmas are caused by:

- Using discretion in an arbitrary, malafide or discriminatory manner
- Nepotism
- Failing to adhere to the requirement of secrecy

Ethical Reasoning: The information technology, globalization, market economies, political conflicts, authority systems and culture have posed several challenges and uncertainties to the public administrators. Western societies and developing countries often experience ethical dilemmas in public governance; hence there is a need for institutional awareness to deal with conflicting values and ethical dilemmas in public services. Everyone is prone to egotism, prejudice, self-justification and self-deception. Only systematic cultivation of fair mindedness, honesty, integrity, self-knowledge and deep concern for the welfare of the others can provide foundations for sound ethical reasoning. Commitment to trust cannot be mandated, it needs to be earned by the individuals.

Values in Public Service

Public servants are guided in their work and their professional conduct by a balanced framework of public service values: democratic, professional, ethical and relationships values. These values are not distinct but overlap and are perspectives from which to observe the universe of Public Service values.

Democratic Values: This is essential to maintain relations between democracy and bureaucracy and particularly in guiding Ministers, under law, to serve the public interest.

- Public servants shall give honest and impartial advice and make all information relevant to a decision available to Ministers.
- Public servants shall loyally implement ministerial decisions, lawfully taken.
- Public servants shall support both individual and collective ministerial accountability and provide legislature and people with information on the results of their work.
- Professional Values: These are required to serve with competence, excellence, efficiency, objectivity and impartiality.
- Public servants must work within the laws of state or country and maintain the tradition of the political neutrality of the Public Service.
- Public servants shall endeavour to ensure the proper, effective and efficient use of public money.
- In the Public Service, how ends are achieved should be as important as the achievements themselves.
- Public servants should constantly renew their commitment to serve people by continually improving the quality of service, by adapting to changing needs through innovation, and by improving the efficiency and effectiveness of government programs and services offered.

- Public servants should also strive to ensure that the value of transparency in government is upheld while respecting their duties of confidentiality under the law.
- These are essential at all times to uphold the public trust.
- Public servants shall perform their duties and arrange their private affairs so that public confidence and trust in the integrity, objectivity and impartiality of government are conserved and enhanced.
- Public servants shall act at all times in a manner that will bear the closest public scrutiny; an obligation that is not fully discharged by simply acting within the law.
- Public servants, in fulfilling their official duties and responsibilities, shall make decisions in the public interest.
- In the event of a conflict between the private interests and the official duties of a public servant, the conflict shall be resolved in favour of the public interest.
- **Values in Relationships:** These are required to demonstrate respect, fairness and courtesy in their dealings with both citizens and fellow public servants.
- Respect for human dignity and the value of every person should always inspire the exercise of authority and responsibility.
- People values should reinforce the wider range of Public Service values. Those who are treated with fairness and civility will be motivated to display these values in their own conduct.
- Public Service departments and organizations should be led through participation, openness and communication and with respect for diversity.
- Appointment decisions in the Public Service shall be based on merit.

- Public Service values should play a key role in recruitment, evaluation and promotion.

Attributes of Ethical Conduct

- Compassion; concern for the well-being of others.
- **Avoidance of Maleficence:** avoiding inflicting suffering and hardship on others.
- **Beneficence:** preventing and alleviating others suffering; meeting the needs of the most vulnerable; promoting others happiness (strongest toward our family and friends).
- Fairness; treating people the way they deserve to be treated; as having equal rights unless merit or need justifies special treatment.

Courage in Opposing Injustice

- Respect for individual autonomy; not manipulating rational individuals even for their own good.
- Respect for the Constitution and other laws enacted by legitimate governing bodies.
- Honesty; not deceiving anyone who deserves to know the truth.
- Not making promises with no intention to keep.
- Keeping promises that are made freely.
- Integrity; upholding obligations inspite of personal inconvenience.

Some Specific Obligations of Public Officials

- Use impartial judgment in the service of all constituents.
- Avoid conflicts of interest that could undermine objective judgment.

- Do not show favoritism toward family and friends in hiring.
- Do not solicit or accept bribes from people seeking to influence your official decisions.
- Do not invest in property or companies that could be affected by your official decisions.

People expect fair and just behaviour from public administrators and servants elected or appointed in view of the power and authority exercised by them, but unfortunately there is a considerable dissatisfaction and discontentment among the citizens. Law and ethical codes cannot alone ensure ethical conduct of public administrators; it requires a supportive environment. There is a dire need for the active and assertive public opinion to create a vibrant and supportive environment to face the non-ethical conduct of the public servants including politicians.

The onus of ethical governance lies primarily on the public servant. Ethics is what one does. It can therefore be conceptualized as a set of actions taken and the overall behavior displayed by the individual public servant. This viewpoint is important since the ethical orientation and behavior of an individual is evaluated against a pre-decided set of values. This behaviour is again scrutinized in terms of issues such as the avoidance, or prevention, harm to others, obedience to and upholding of the law that governs ethical actions. Such scrutiny has a bearing on the overall performance of the system.

All this poses important questions that need to be answered. Chief among them is the question whether ethics should be taught early enough in schools and subsequently in colleges and universities that it forms the bedrock of decision making further on. An understanding of the principles of ethics complements the existing values, that are already deeply instilled in individuals, with the influences around them.

The link between ethics and behaviour is brought to the fore once again on account of the prevalence of ethical orientation in the individuals. This serves as a moral compass and helps in the changing of belief systems and the inherent approach to making ethical decisions. The underlying assumption here is that, in the absence of such a compass, or ethical framework, the default course certainly would be an unethical one. If the prevalent atmosphere is one that is characteristed by many deviations from normality and one in which there is no opposition to morally deviant actions, clearly, then, unethical behavior can easily become the norm. One way to rectify such a situation is to infuse into the environment a native respect for rectitude and integrity. That can bring about a change in the environment and create a positive influence at the workplace that would place emphasis on positive behaviour in line with accepted mores of morals and ethics. This will again serve as a feedback mechanism for the leadership to adopt an improved approach to creating an ethically compliant environment.

1.7 Individual Values

Public servants confront ethical and unethical realities on a daily basis and employees in this domain are vulnerable to ethical lapses. Individual values play a crucial role in instilling beliefs concerning ethical orientations in individual public servants. Shared values among the public servants could be developed based on idealized notions of honour, respect and responsibility. Moreover, many public servants pride themselves on values such as conscientiousness, integrity, dedication and competence. This feeling is useful in the process of institution-building in which ethics are given due importance - where individuals are proud of their work accept accountability and commit themselves to the greater good - to compliance with relevant rules, regulation and guidelines.

1.8 Dealing with Dilemmas in Administration

When confronted with the fundamental question what to do and how to act in complex situations, and to the extent that contrasted values or decisional premises could apply in the situation, one is entering the world of ethical dilemmas or that of 'hard choices' (Hart, 1961). A dilemma is something wider and more demanding than a problem, however difficult or complex the latter may be (Rapport, 1960). The reason is that dilemmas, unlike problems, cannot be solved in the terms in which they are initially presented to the decision-maker.

A dilemma can be best dealt if the terms of reference are altered and the whole situation is reformulated and redefined so that full account is taken and due respect paid to every stakeholder's opinion, which are then ordered and linked among themselves in a more systematic and coherent manner.

The advanced set of fundamental principles or criteria that integrate and rearrange the process of dealing with ethical dilemmas in public administration are: (i) Democratic **A**ccountability of Administration, (ii) the Rule of **L**aw and the Principle of **L**egality, (iii) Professional **I**ntegrity and (iv) **R**esponsiveness to Civil Society.

The **ALIR** (from the initials of key notions) forms something similar to Tailcoat Parsons' (1964) 'evolutionary universals' as far as public administration is concerned. As a matter of fact, both sets of concepts bear a close resemblance and may even be considered as complementary to one another. Taking into account of previous hypothesis about the underlying convergence between the Parsonian concept of 'evolutionary universals' and the ALIR imperatives of ethical reasoning expounded here, we may at this point reach a preliminary conclusion about good governance and the moral standards obtaining in it. Such a type of governance and administration would, therefore, have to be democratic, bound to the rule of law, capable of carrying out its missions and tasks efficiently and effectively and be responsive to civil society.

(i) The imperative of Accountability

The distinction between politics and administration, which forms one of the most classic doctrines of modem political science and public administration (Wilson, 1887), connotes not only their division of functions and their structural separation but also the subordination of the latter to the former. Thus, the primacy of politics in the politico-administrative nexus explains the ultimate political or rather governmental control of the administrative machinery of the state in a democracy. The loyalty of the bureaucracy to its political masters is grounded on the obligation of ministers in parliamentary democracies to be answerable and responsible to the legislature (ministerial responsibility to Parliament). It is only by that means that the representatives of the nation may hold the bureaucracy accountable to the will of the people and the general interest (volontiginirale).

Since it is ministers who are accountable to Parliament, not civil servants, it follows that the latter are obliged to execute the orders of the former even if they disagree with their content, provided that they originate from a legitimate source of authority in the institutional hierarchy, and that authority insists on being executed despite the remonstrance put forward by officials. Subordination of civil servants to elected representatives who act as law-makers and policy-setters forms a *sine qua* non precondition of democratic politics. Unless subordinated to political control the bureaucracy and administration usurps power, which doe not belong to it; if that happens the bureaucracy (civil or military) enters the political arena, undermines representative democracy and subjugates politics and government to its own interests and commands.

It is then a fundamental ethical duty bearing on civil servants in pluralist parliamentary democracies to subordinate them to political authority. Hence they owe a duty of loyalty and faithfulness to the duly elected or appointed political masters, however transient they may be. In the same vein they would have to show a spirit of neutrality and discretion in their official capacity as members of the administrative infrastructure of the state vis-à-vis partisan politics, and keep at bay their own personal preferences in the performance of their duties and responsibilities.

The conclusion that may be drawn is that 'democratic virtue' does form part and parcel of the core values and normative determinants of administrative behaviour in the public sector: namely, the administration should be held accountable to government and parliament on matters of policy and expediency. It should, however, also be stressed that the supremacy of politics over the administration in the constitutional division of powers does not amount to and cannot be taken to mean the politicization of public services and the state bureaucracy, because that would then undermine the instrumental value of the executive branch of government and administration. Administrators, although guided by and subordinated to politicians, are not their clients or servants in the partisan sense of the term. That would well have been the case in the context of the spoils system that prevailed in administrative practices in many a country in the past. Modem governance and administration, in contrast, is founded on the idea that the differentiation of roles and functions between politics and administration increases the quality and potential of either of them. In that regard, 'speaking truth to power' can be considered as a vital ingredient of professional ethics and moral integrity of civil servants and the administrative machinery of the state in general.

(ii) The imperative of Legality

The rule of law, (Rechtstaat, Etat de Droit) besides being one of the fundamental evolutionary universals in both modem politics and society pertains in a very specific and significant way to administrative conduct. Respect and adherence to the principle of legality manifests a spirit of constitutionalism and forms an essential prerequisite for the legitimacy of state action and the exercise of authority; thus, it was regarded by Max Weber as providing the third type of legitimation of authority (charismatic, traditional, legal-rational).

Respect for and application of the principle of legality entails a particular type of control on administrative action that aims to see that public administration operates within the context of the law established by the legislature (Parliament). Since the source of all power is ultimately the people, according to the fundamental constitutional principle of popular sovereignty that is enshrined in most democracies nowadays, it follows that all power must be exercised in the name of and in the general interest of the people. Consequently, government and administration alike as the executive branch of the state and indirectly of the nation itself have to respect the law, which is the expression of the will of the nation. In this sense, originating from the constitutional tradition of the French revolution, the state could be seen as no more than the mechanism which the nation set up for its own governance and administration. And for that to take place in an effective rather than an arbitrary manner, the running of the business of the state has to be guided and determined by an articulate system of laws and rules. Their artful application in concrete cases by administrative or judicial authorities then forms the essence of the principle of legality and the rule of law.

The control of legality of administrative action, initially exercised by the administration itself and ultimately by independent courts of justice, purports to ensure, in particular,that proper procedures have been followed and observed, as well as that equity, reasonableness and impartiality have been respected. It can then be argued and with good cause be expected that the artful application of the principle of legality in administrative performance would serve and promote the rule of law and the avoidance of abuse of power (Wade, 1977; Rivero, 1980; Jowell, 1985; Spiliotopoulos, 1991).

The idea that people should be governed by law rather than by fiat is, of course, germane both to democracy and modernity. It could also be said that law establishes what may be described as the minimum standard of morality. Usually, unethical conduct - be it bribery, theft, favoritism, abuse of power, etc. - consists of a violation of law, that is putting someone above or beyond the law. Thus, consistent and fair enforcement of law can be a first priority of an ethics reform strategy. Even in antiquity, however, the concept of justice, in which all virtue is consummated, according to Philosopher Aristotle, required that people should recognize the sovereignty of law, not of other humans - the implication being that the legitimately established system of laws should be allowed to rule freely. Thus, Solon abandoned power after establishing a set of rules for his native city-state of Athens in the sixth century BC. What he intended to declare by this example was the value of respect for the law in itself, and that people should be ruled by law, not by themselves, otherwise he would be a tyrant, not a legislator.

(iii) The imperative of Integrity

The application of knowledge and science in public affairs has been historically related to the advent of and increase in professionalism in their exercise. However relative or tentative that may occasionally have proven to be, it is nonetheless the case that a 'profession of government' (Chapman, 1959) has taken shape in Europe and elsewhere. Thus, the notion of public administration is usually inclusive of all public services exercising authority in accordance with public law and under the overall guidance and direction of politically responsible ministers or other elected officials at the central, regional or local level; in order to carry out their functions public agencies employ personnel having the status of public officers and are thereof governed by special provisions for recruitment, career, discipline and control. Professional integrity and autonomy - the 'professional virtue', as we may call it - qualifying absolute hierarchical subordination entails that public administration may be brought under political guidance and control but its staff is recruited and serve under the authority of law and in the public interest, and not on the basis of partisan favoritism.

The state's 'guardian elite' (Argyriades, 1996) is comprised of the body of civil servants, permanent officers subordinate to ministers who are responsible to Parliament. Civil servants are supposed to be fully competent on the basis of their ascertained knowledge, experience and expertise, and independent enough to offer official advice to ministers as well as to implement public policies and decisions in an efficient and effective manner in the public interest. To that end the essential features of the distinct profession of government and administration have, from a historical and comparative perspective, proven to be as follows:

(a) Recruitment should take place on the basis of merit ascertained by special tests which are administered by assigned independent authorities so that entry to the service is no longer subject to spoils system practices (clientelism, favoritism, patronage). Thus, meritocracy becomes an important precondition of professional integrity and autonomy.

(b) Disciplinary measures should be taken by the service's own councils promoting a corporate spirit (esprit de corps) and self-government in the administrative profession; promotion on the career ladder should also be based on seniority (to the extent that longer service testifies wider experience) and merit (after rating and evaluation of performance).

(c) Continuity of tenure of service and exclusiveness of practice in the designated field; that of course may be reserved for the necessary number of permanent civil servants whose duties and responsibilities involve either exercise of powers conferred by public law or/and safeguarding the general interests of the state. There could be exclusion from this category of those employed on a contractual basis (unestablished staff).

(d) Training and education should increase professionalism in government and administration as a whole; i.e., involving not only its legal or juridical aspects ('juristenmonopol') but also other branches and fields of executive action (engineers, doctors, economists, etc.).

(e) There should also be a special set of rights and obligations promoting loyalty and integrity, including neutrality of practice; namely, a readiness to serve different legitimate governments regardless of one's personal preferences or choices.

Professionalism in public service could then be seen to accrue from a combination of knowledge, of expertise, of judgment and conduct in accordance with standards, as well as commitment to the field. Competence on the basis of knowledge, experience and expertise is in all established professions (doctors, lawyers, engineers, accountants, journalists, academics, etc.) usually accompanied by a set of shared values held by peers on how to use and apply this knowledge.

That is to say, knowledge and expertise would have to be used with certain standards defining professional ethics such as, for instance, avoiding corruption in the delivery of services. Otherwise, the profession is deprived of an essential precondition of its claim to legitimacy. As Hegel supremely put it:

What the service of the state really requires is that men shall forego the selfish and capricious satisfaction of their subjective ends; by this very sacrifice, they acquire the right to find their satisfaction in, but only in, the dutiful discharge of their public functions. In this fact, so far as public business is concerned, lies the link between universal and particular interests which constitutes both the concept of the state and its inner stability.

In this respect, the profession of government's administration and, to a comparable extent, the more recent profession of public management would be accompanied by a code of ethics consolidating professional virtue and integrity, and increasing morale and self-confidence. This is indeed often the case in many an administrative system in various countries. The imperative for integrity constitutes, therefore, a source of internal self-control in administrative conduct based on ethical standards and criteria shared and respected by the corps of professional administrators. Avoiding, for instance, corruption and exhibiting integrity would then be for them a matter of personal and professional honour and prestige in a culture of ethics, and not simply an externally imposed obligation. We may, therefore, conclude that the professional virtue for civil servants would impose on them certain rather austere standards and would require that they uphold and respect them in their conduct. 'Integer vitae sclerisque pours' (integrity in life and pure from crime), as Horace put it in one of his Odes, would then seem to offer an appropriate definition of the ethical imperative for public servants.

(iv) The imperative of Responsiveness

For Hegel, public functionaries were the servants of the state only, not of civil society, since it was the former that expressed the general will of the people. The latter – Burgerliche Gesellshaft - on the contrary, was seen by Hegel as a conglomerate of particular and inconsistent wishes and interests. This then became the sphere of the particular group of persons with their own private systems of needs and the efforts to satisfy them. Whereas the state served the general interest, civil society was the state of partial interests.

In this somehow dichotomous idea of social construction, individuals actualize themselves while partaking in various activities in civil society and 'in becoming something definite, i.e. something specifically particularized' (Hegel, 1967: 133). The state, however, with its system of governance and law provides the underlying conditions by which individuals and their actions may find their fullest fulfillment. For that reason, the state was for Hegel the 'actuality of the ethical idea', that is the unity of the universal and the particular.

Hegel's thesis could be more readily understood if account is taken of the fact that he lived in a country where most citizens were simply 'subjects', without participation in the work of government, and where, therefore, a political life and tradition, like the English, was almost wholly lacking. His book was an attempt to educate Germans beyond 'civil' to 'political' life (Hegel, 1967: 376).

Almost 200 years later we are now in a position to know that, unless there is an articulate and independent civil society, no political life and even less democratic polity is likely to grow and flourish. That is why civil society has been declared as one of the most essential preconditions of liberty and democracy (Geliner, 1996; Argyriades, 1998). The new prevailing idea by the turn of the 21st century is that the state should neither command civil society nor be subservient to it; instead it would cooperate in building social capital to the benefit of the human community concerned. Thus, balancing a responsive state and an active civil society presents as an optimal strategy for enhancing the quality of and prospects for democracy.

In this respect, the 'civic virtue' of ethical reasoning in state action entails that public institutions be responsive to society and pay attention to the needs and demands of the people, facilitating access to services and creating an enabling environment for sustainable human and social development. Responsiveness is not restricted to market forces but also and even primarily concerns citizens' participation in all levels and layers of government, as well as empowering people in human communities (Bovens, 1998). Responsiveness also entails consultation in governance and the promotion of a kind of 'communicative ethic' (Habermas, 1987) in societal affairs. The transition, however cumbersome it may be, from the command type of authority over people to more communicative types of reasoning and administration of things seems to emerge as a paradigm shift in societal affairs radicalizing the features of modernity in our times.

In this context, civil society not only furnishes the state with needs and demands of an individual nature, but also with valuable sources of information, feedback, criticism and evaluation of performance. Therefore, notions like decentralization, de-bureaucratization, privatization and citizen participation loom large in the repertoire of reform programmes and practices of many contemporary administrative systems, and affect the interface between civil society and the state. It is not only that citizens have increased their voice as taxpayers and customers of public services demanding value for money; citizens and civil societies are also seen to be acting as watchdogs to the state's performance. Society is no longer at the mercy of state authority and control by the bureaucracy, rather the latter is under society's watchful eye (Buchanan, 1985).

In this sense, the imperative for responsiveness to civil society calls for an increased awareness and readiness to adapt to changing values and conditions in society at large, and stresses the need for an overall 'external' or societal accountability of state authorities and administration.

Naturally, 'a country's view of public administration reflects its underlying philosophy of society and of the state' (Chapman, 1959: 309). State officials are affected by the way the public at large regards them. Eventually, civil servants forming a middle-class profession, par excellence, acquire the features that society expects of them. Public administration forms a partial regime in the societal framework; it is part of the state, which is subject to a distinct 'ethic of responsibility' - in the Weberian sense - vis-a-vis society.

2. GOVERNANCE

Governance can be defined as the way of governing people. Effective governance not only requires institutional and government reforms, but also, reforms in market mechanisms for service delivery of public goods. Developing community voice and, considering and acknowledging people's mindset, will act as a means to achieve the principles of good governance. Good Governance is not a stand alone entity, but a process that should be adopted and integrated with every essence of life and in every possible sphere.

2.1 Governance: A Holistic View

We hold these truths to be self-evident, that all men are created equal, that they are endowed by their Creator with certain inalienable Rights, that among these are Life, Liberty and the pursuit of Happiness.

- United States Declaration of Independence

As stated earlier, Governance can be defined as the way of governing people. Different scholars have defined the term in a number of ways. For instance- "Governance is not merely about ownership but about running the institution for the optimal benefit of all its stakeholders. Governance has a powerful influence on ethical behaviour because it defines the value system of the institution. Governance is a problem that all of our society must resolve if we are not to decline into a wholly lawless and criminal society. Governance is about governing; it is not merely about ownership. Even an owner has to learn to govern. Good governance implies that the institution is run for the optimal benefit of the stakeholders in it. It implies also that it is not merely the short term well being of the institution, it must be prepared for its long term growth in a changing environment" (Rao S.L., 2000).

The World Bank defines 'Governance' as "the traditions and institutions by which authority is exercised for the common good".

This narrow definition has raised a lot of debate on the essence of governance; which is much beyond what we understand as 'government'. Therefore effective governance not only requires institutional and government reforms, but also reforms in market mechanisms for service delivery of public goods. Empowering the community, responding to the people's mindset, and engaging in the Public Private Partnership (PPP) mode of governance with citizens as partners rather than as beneficiaries, are some features of an effective system of governance.

Good Governance

Accountability and transparency are important parameters of good governance. Decision making in achieving good governance must always, at all levels, include the stakeholders, be they gainers or losers. Good governance must also ensure active involvement and participation of community in implementing the decisions taken. Besides, the whole arena of governance also does take into account the way of governing formal and informal structures and resources. Therefore, governance is not government in itself, but the process adopted for decision-making and implementation.

The end of twentieth century witnessed good governance as a buzz-word attracting attention of the knowledge, administrative, research and management domain. Besides the World Bank discussing 'Government and Development', the IMF also highlighted issues in governance in one of their documents. The concept of SMART (Small-Moral-Accountable-Responsive-Transparent) governance gradually paved the way for conceptualizing good governance. Development, at all stages, necessitates good governance as its means.

E-governance

The process of governance involves continuous interaction of the State, with formal and informal enterprises and civil society. The advent of Information and Communication Technology (ICT) has significantly influenced these interactions; converting the process of good governance to e-governance. Therefore, e-governance refers to the rational and effective use of IT, in order to improve the existing system of governance rendering it more approachable and accessible to people.

Recognized Areas of Governance

Good Governance is not a stand alone entity, but a process that should be adopted and integrated with every aspect of life. Yet till date, only a few areas have been recognized for the application of practices of good governance, viz., society, politics and institutions. Now, to understand the superstructure of good governance in each of these areas, we need to look deep into its different dimensions, some of which are discussed below.

Societal Governance

Governance in a society is guided by behavior of the community with respect to its environment, individuals, institutional frameworks and Society. Therefore it is essential for the community to have and share certain standards of ethics and values. The binding factor of ethics and values in governing Society should be such as to encourage the belief that any anti-social behavior is unethical and corrupt, even if such behavior is practiced by persons in power.

In order to inculcate ethics into a Society, it is very important to bring in participation of people in practicing those ethics. The prime agenda of governance is to put people at its focus and empower them, which is only possible through active and voluntary participation of people. In other words, participation is an important aspect of empowerment in any society. Therefore ensuring participation of people in practicing ethical behavior, which is the ultimate objective of governance in developing a society, can be achieved as an 'end', by using it as a 'means' in itself.

The above mentioned procedure of societal governance converges into the widely acknowledged idea of a self-governing society, where people govern themselves. According to Cruickshank, 1996, "Governance in this case is something we do to ourselves, not something done to us by those in power"; therefore we empower ourselves. Individual empowerment is possible by putting in a cumulative effort towards building a local organization with access to information and local resource pool, which will ensure that empowerment, through participation, is inclusive in nature. This will, in course of time, pave the way for good societal governance through empowered citizens and a government that is accountable.

Political Governance

Good governance in the political arena not only involves the constitution of a sound parliamentary committee but also free interaction with policy and decision makers, research scholars and think tanks, so as to engage in a healthy debate regarding directing development of the country and its people. Political parties must be transparent in their views, opinions and objectives; more than that, they must be accountable to people. Political leaders and other people in power may decide, but not supersede public opinion; therefore good political governance should empower the citizens.

Moreover, since good governance is the process of governing, good political governance in a society, or in a nation, should be a continuous process, not a discreet agenda initiated only before elections for good image of the parties. Agenda of political parties should be free from personal bias or any kind of vested interests, and the same should clearly spell out the interests of the commons. Hence the inculcation of values and ethics are not only restricted to societal governance, but also should be deeply articulated in political governance.

While political parties, leaders and their role form one part of the story in political governance, the framework of the legislative system (laws, rules, regulations, penalties, etc.) forms another part of the story. Besides having a strong Parliamentary Committee, political governance can be firmly backed by fair and just laws, rules and regulations inclusive of all sections in the society and, provision of strict and adequate punishments.

Political governance should witness a shift from its traditional top-down approach of bureaucracy to the grassroots bottom-up approach. There is no doubt denying the fact that bureaucrats, as administrators, will exist in order to run the society, but what is good for the masses, should be looked at from the viewpoint of the people.

Corporate Governance

Corporate Governance can be defined as an ongoing practice of adaptation, refinement and adjustment, which requires systemic and periodic review of the progressive works in the institution. Good corporate governance directs a firm or an institution towards better and ethical behavioural patterns, and also to a fair framework of institutional governance. Therefore, corporate governance can be understood in broad aspects: firstly with regard to firm behaviour in terms of ethics, values, performance, efficiency, work and finance structure meant for both internal staff and external clients; and with regard to the framework of the governance involving operation rules and codes, transparency in information sharing, etc. Adoption of good corporate governance as a means, will not only lead to its success, but will also provide a sense of security and belonging to all the internal and external stakeholders, by continuous value addition.

Not much was known about corporate governance before the second half of the twentieth century. It was the United States that initiated research on theoretical and practical aspects of corporate governance; followed by the other countries like Japan, Germany and United Kingdom. Gradually the emerging concept spread to the developing countries.

It was the WTO that first developed international standards and codes for corporate governance across nations, followed by the World Bank and the OECD. Later on, almost all the Regional Development banks and UN Agencies had set up corporate governance codes and guidelines. Initiatives of so many agencies led to formulation of a large number of such codes and guidelines, but the overall motive of all of them was common; they aimed at achieving the independence of the board, roles and responsibilities of shareholders and, transparency and accountability in the organization.

In spite of the circulated standards, codes and guidelines, there have been issues in corporate governance mainly because the ownership of management and ownership of control has been separated in the present day institutions. The external regulatory and supervisory authorities like The Comptroller and Auditor General of India, Chief Vigilance Commissioner, GoI, and The Reserve Bank of India etc. have a significant role to play in this context.

The Essence of Governance

Governance, as a process, goes hand in hand with the growth and development of a nation. Good governance has to be realized in all socio-economic, political, cultural and demographic aspects of life for individuals and, regulatory, administrative, legislative and executive bodies, at all levels. The process of governing, so imbibed and inculcated, influences ethics and values in every sphere of life. Therefore more the transparency and accountability, greater is the inception of moral values of honesty, dedication, effectiveness and inclusiveness; thereby realizing the essence of good governance.

2.2 Governance in India- A Brief Historical Account

Governance, in the form of administration, has existed in India since early historical times. Consolidation of empires in history began in the Mauryan era, followed by the Mughal era and the British Rule in India. Many features of modern-day governance are similar to that of these periods.

Evolution

Ancient History

In the beginning of the Vedic age people did not have a settled life and were nomads. But with development in agriculture people started to settle down in groups. The organization was mainly tribal and the head of the tribe was the Raja or the King, though the concept of King had yet not developed. With the passage of time large kingdoms started to grow and by the 6th century BC there were 16 Mahajanapadas (Kingdoms). There were many small republics also in ancient India. These republics had some elements of democracy in their administration. The king (raja) was the supreme head of the legislative, executive and judiciary branches. He was assisted in administration by a number of officials. The members of the Council of Ministers could give advice to the king, but final decisions were left to the king. The ministers and other officials were directly appointed by the king.

Medieval History

During the Mauryan period there existed both civil and military officials. There were officials who maintained the records of population, income and expenditure of government, etc. We find reference to officials and clerks who collected income tax and custom duties. Spy system was an important feature of Mauryan administration. The empire was divided into many provinces and each one of these provinces was governed by a Governor and Council of Ministers. In the provinces there were local officials called Rajukas, who became more powerful during the reign of King Ashoka. There were some departments which decided certain important matters of administration. There existed a standing army which was again controlled by certain committees.

Administration during the Gupta period was universally acclaimed as the Swarna Yuga (Golden Period). During the Gupta period the administration was more or less like that of the Mauryas. In the Gupta administration, the governors of the provinces were more independent as compared to the Mauryans, where the administration was highly centralized.

Kautilya's Arthashastra

Kautilya, the architect of Mauryan Empire, wrote 'Arthashastra' in the 4th Century B.C. and is the first known Indian treatise on Public administration. Arthashastra is "the science which deals with the acquisition and protection of the means of livelihood. At the same time, it is a means of ensuring the well-being of man in general. It has a two-fold aim. The first, refers to the administration and protection of the state i.e., 'palana' and the second, is the conquest of territory i.e., 'labha'. It is the science of politics and administration. Thus, the science of polity is a combination of science of wealth" (Vajiram et.al. 2013) and art of governance.

The 'Arthashastra' compiles 15 books on both theory of Public Administration and its practice. 'Tantra' or internal administration is dealt in the first five books. Kautilya, though not a founder of theories of administration, has elaborated and put forward many real life examples of administrative aspects in all his books.

Being a believer in the role of a king as a public servant, Kautilya threw light on the Social Contract Theory to describe origin of state in the Arthashastra. Kautilya mentions on origin of state that, "In order to protect people from '*matsya nyaya*' (big fish eating small), a king was made by the people by agreeing to pay taxes in order to protect their wellbeing". Kautilya has accepted Monarchy as the norm and says is the best form when compared to the joint rule over whole kingdom (Dvairajya) or a rule by foreign ruler (Vairajya). Arthashastra strongly rejects the rule by a foreigner because a foreign ruler would have no genuine interest in the welfare of the conquered state and was likely to deplete its men and resources which was later proved right by many of nationalists during freedom struggle with regard to plunder of wealth by the British.

Kautilya proposes the 'Saptanga doctrine', where he mentions of seven vital organs of the state or 'prakritis', which are:

- The 'Svamin' or the Ruler
- The 'Amatya' or Minister
- The 'Janapada' or Territory with people settled on it
- The 'Durga' or Fortified capital
- The 'Kosh' or Treasury
- The 'Danda' or the Army
- The 'Mitra' or Ally or Friend

All the seven organs represent the seven pillars of a state. All the 'Prakritis' are inter-related, and if any negative aspect develops in any one of them, then there will be an impact on all the others. The king, being at the centre of these Prakritis, will have to depend on all of them for efficient administration.

Though Arthashastra considers King as the pivot and gives him extensive powers, at the same time it mentions that the foremost duty of king is protection of the subjects and their property i.e., welfare of the people which was called as 'Rakshana' or 'Palana'. Protection is both from natural calamities and anti-social elements.

Arthashastra mentions that the king should take part actively in war and administration, facilitate trade, build bridges and should act like a father at the time of natural calamities. The king is also the protector of social order by preserving the Vedic social order. There was also a mention of those who have to be maintained by the state like minors, aged and distressed. Therefore, each activity or duty of king mentioned in the Arthashastra talks about welfare of the people. Hence, 'Arthashastra' state is neither a police state nor merely a tax-gathering state, but a 'Welfare State'.

Kautilya considered moral values as means to prosperity in this world and to paving the way to heaven after death. He asserted, "For the world, when maintained in accordance with the Vedas, will ever prosper and not perish. Therefore, the king shall never allow the people to swerve from their dharma". He added, "For, when adharma overwhelms dharma, the King himself will be destroyed". The insights contained in the Arthashastra are as relevant today as they were in his time and thus make it an ageless contribution. He truly possessed a modern outlook in formulating such universally relevant principles.

According to Kautilya's Arthashastra, a ruler should follow public welfare.

"Prajasukhe sukhamrajya prajanam chahite hitam
Natmapriyyam hitam rajanaha prajanam cha hitam priyam"

(In the happiness of his public rests the king's happiness, in their welfare his welfare. He shall not consider as good only that which pleases him but treats as beneficial to him whatever pleases his public.)

The Mughal Administration

With a subsequent impact in the later stages of history, the Muslim conquest of India is a worthy example of consolidation of empire under the rule of Akbar. The consolidation happened in 1556, after the Battle of Panipat. The death of Aurangzeb brought in the end of Mughal Empire in 1707, not ignoring the fact that the empire was still run by subsequent puppet emperors till 1862.

Prior to the Mughals, though there was good administration under Sher Shah Suri's rule, but no systematic mention of 'Principles of Administration' at vertical hierarchical level. Unlike other Mughal rulers, Akbar's successors, more or less followed his mentioned patterns.

The delimitation and demarcation of various units of administration as also the clear enunciation of the rights and duties of the various heads of administration were a remarkable contribution of Akbar. Our knowledge of administrative pattern during Akbar's time is derived mainly from the 'Ain-i-Akbari', a supplement to the official chronicle of his reign which consists of a selection of documents illustrating the Emperor's activities in each department of administration. The Mughals imported certain foreign elements into their administrative system. They came to India from Central Asia where they had their own system of administration. In India, they modified the same according to Indian traditions.

The concept and traditions of Kautilya's 'organs of state' influenced the political and administrative approach of the Mughals. The basic features were an authoritarian centre with the Emperor symbolizing the State alongside an extensive and efficient administration for the purpose of law enforcement and revenue collection. Practice of fair justice was evident.

In the Mughal Empire, the Emperor was wielding absolute power, holding his Will as the law and the Empire was established on military lines.

A critical look on the reasons for failure of the Mughal Empire, shows that the absence of democratic features and lack of introspection on the part of the rulers were the principle causes therefore.

Yet the Mughals succeeded in building a homogenous governance system in the country, with uniformity of administration over a vast territory - a system that was rich in many aspects. That system could not, however, establish a nation or a state with stable identity. Ultimately a weakening central government and the impact of rebellions and wars resulted in the Empire being humbled by the British conquerors.

Modern History

The modern history of India roughly began with the end of the Mughal Empire. After the last strong Mughal Emperor Aurangzeb died. India was fragmented into a number of small petty kingdoms. There was chaos and confusion all over the country with almost every other king fighting for control of territories. This attracted foreigners who promptly came to India by establishing trade links and draining away our resources. The Europeans were particularly interested in spice trade with India while the Dutch monopolized this area. This led to a series of interesting changes in the Indian sub-continent.

The British came to know of the abundant resources in India and the trade links with other countries. The 17th century saw fierce competition between different European companies. By the end of the 18th century, the British conquered all and established their company in India. Gradually, they acquired political power and secured a strong place in the administrative affairs of the country. They established themselves firmly over the Indian subcontinent and brought about many changes in political, economic and social aspects of the country.

After the end of the First World War, British imperialism has taken further deeper roots in India giving raise to nationwide agitations against the British rule. By the end of 19th century, the Indians formed their own political party called Indian National Congress which worked with the British for the benefits of the Indians. The British did not acknowledge the needs of the Indians and Congress and slowly the Congress turned against them.

British Rule in India

British rule over India changed the course of history of India. The British came to India at the start of the seventeenth century. This was the time when the British East India Company was established in India to break the Dutch monopoly over spice trade.

Legacy of the British Rule

During East India company's rule, governance in British India began with the initiatives of Thomas Babington Macaulay who presented an impassioned argument before the Parliament about the future role of British governance in India. Macaulay asserted that India cannot have representative institutions like in Europe and the role of the British colonizers should be to give good government to people based on a rule of law but not a free government.

The British rule in India has formed the base of our present Indian administrative structure. In India, the British period of administration is divided into the following parts, East India Company's (EIC) rule (up to 1857) and, the British rule (from 1858 up to 1947). The revolution of 1857 brought an end of East India Company rule, and the British Government assumed direct control.

Salient Features of the Company Rule

As the company began to transform itself from a commercial concern into a territorial power, there was a corresponding change in the attitude of British Parliament towards it by establishing a Board of Control to regulate activities of the Company. The successive legislations brought forward many changes. The net result of all these enactments was the emergence of a highly centralized British administration in India.

Out of the many features of the Company Rule, the salient ones are very well documented; the following paragraphs reflect these features:

Provinces: The Provinces came into existence in British India first before the Central Government.

The Governor-General: The office of Governor-General became the symbol of centralization.

The Legislature, the Executive and the Judiciary: The Regulating Act, 1773 established a Supreme Court with a Chief Justice and 3 other judges to be appointed by the King. Thus, provision was made for all the activities of the State - executive i.e., Governor-General, legislative i.e., Council and Judicial, and the foundations of a new system of governance were laid.

The Civil Service: The origin of civil services distinguished the civilian personnel from the military. Gradually the right of Patronage disappeared and merit-based civil service started with the introduction of open competition as method of recruitment by the Charter Act of 1853.

Wellesley started the first college of Fort William in Calcutta in 1800 after realizing that the civil servants need to be well acquainted with the languages, laws and customs of the people, and at the same time be well informed on the British Constitution and be well versed in ethics, civil jurisprudence, the laws of nations and general history.

Decentralized Administration: The District was an important unit of administration since the Mauryan era and the British continued the importance given to the district. A District Collector was first appointed by Warren Hastings in 1772. By 1786, the district came to occupy a central place in the scheme of local administration.

Impact of the British rule

India under the British rule witnessed a series of changes after the Revolt of 1857. The British Rule had an extensive impact on Indian administration, as evident from the contemporary Indian Administrative structure.

The Indian administration under the British rule, witnessed a series of changes through experiments and innovations. As in case of the Mughals, the British rule also tried to uphold certain traditions of their previous rule and administration, thus paving the way of continuity of all the good aspects of administration and governance in the country.

Indian National Congress

The Indian National Congress was founded in the year 1885. The first session of Congress was presided over by Womesh Chandra Bonnerjee who was also elected as the first president of Indian National Congress party. Around seventy reputed delegates that included educationalists, lawyers, journalists etc. attended the first session of the congress when it was established.

One of the primary and severe outbursts of resentment against the British rule came in the form of the Indian revolt of 1857. This revolt followed the battles of Plassey and Buxar and the main cause was resentment against setting up of British rule in Bengal. It is called the first war of independence by many historians though it is a debatable topic.

2.3 Governance of the State - Independent India

Introduction

Constitution - the fountainhead of Governance

Governance of the State, like any other organization, is a creature of a set of laws. A constitution is a body of principles that determine nature of the State. It is a fundamental document according to which different parts of the State function. A Constitution is the basic document that defines and delimits the powers of various organs of the State.

The Constitution of India is the supreme law of India. It lays down the framework defining fundamental political principles, establishes the structure, procedures, powers, and duties of government institutions, and sets out fundamental rights, directive principles, and the duties of citizens.

Evolution of the Constitution of India

Evolution of the Constitution of India can be traced back from an in-depth understanding of the provisions under the following Acts: Government of India Act 1858, Indian Councils Act 1861, Indian Councils Act 1892, Indian Councils Act 1909, Government of India Act 1919, Government of India Act 1935 and Indian Independence Act 1947.

"The Constitution of India is the supreme law of India. The Constitution was adopted by the Indian Constituent Assembly on 26 November 1949, and came into effect on 26 January 1950. The date of 26 January was chosen to com-memorate the Purna Swaraj declaration or the declaration of the independence of India, 1930. With its adoption, the Union of India officially became the modern and contemporary Republic of India and it replaced the Government of India Act 1935 as the country's fundamental governing document. To ensure constitutional autochthony, the framers of constitution inserted Article 395 in the constitution and by this Article the Indian Inde-pendence Act, 1947 was repealed. The constitution declares India to be a sovereign, socialist, secular, democratic republic, assuring its citizens of justice, equality, and liberty, and endeavors to promote fraternity among them. The words "socialist" and "secular" were added to the definition in 1976 by constitutional amendment (mini constitution). India celebrates the adoption of the constitution on 26 January each year as the Republic Day. Besides the English version, there is an official Hindi translation of the constitution. Dr. Bhimrao Ramji Ambedkar is widely regarded as the father of the Indian Constitution". (Wikipedia, accessed on 02/05/2014)

Drafting of the Constitution

The Constituent Assembly, constituted to document the constitution of India, initiated its work with the formation of various Committees in its meeting held on 14 August 1947. These committees included the Committee on Fundamental Rights, the Union Powers Committee and the Union Constitution Committee.

On 29 August 1947, the Drafting Committee was constituted, with Dr B. R. Ambedkar as the Chairman along with six other members assisted by a constitutional advisor. These members were Pandit Govind Ballabh Pant, Kanaiyalal Maneklal Munshi (K M Munshi, formerly the Home Minister, Bombay), Alladi Krishnaswamy Iyer (formerly the Advocate General, Madras State), N Gopalaswami Ayengar (formerly the Prime Minister, J&K and later a member of the Nehru Cabinet), B L Mitter (formerly the Advocate General, India), Md. Saadullah (formerly the Chief Minister of Assam) and D P Khaitan (scion of the Khaitan business family and a renowned lawyer). The constitutional advisor was Sir Benegal Narsing Rau (who became the First Indian Judge in the International Court of Justice, 1950–54). Later B L Mitter resigned and was replaced by Madhav Rao (Legal Advisor of Maharaja of Vadodara). Owing to the death of D P Khaitan, T T Krishnamachari was included in the Committee.

A draft Constitution was prepared by the Committee and submitted to the Assembly on the 4 November 1947. The Assembly met in sessions open to the public for 166 days, spread over a period of 2 years, 11 months and 18 days before adopting the Constitution, The Draft constitution was debated and over 2000 amendments were moved over a period of two years. 308 members of the Assembly signed two copies of the document. Finally, on 26 Nov. 1949, the process was completed and Constituent Assembly adopted the constitution. 284 members signed the document (one each in Hindi and English) on 24 January 1950 and the process of constitution making was complete.

Rs.1, 00, 00,000 was the official estimate of expenditure on the Constituent Assembly.

The original Constitution of India is hand-written with beautiful calligraphy, each page beautified and decorated by artists from Shantiniketan including Beohar Ram Manohar Sinha and Nandalal Bose. On the 26 of January 1950, the Constitution of India became the law of all the States and territories of India.

International influence on the Constitution

The framers of the constitution borrowed provisions form several sources and many other constitutions of the world. They were most heavily influenced by the British model of parliamentary democracy. In addition, a number of principles were adopted from the Constitution of the United States of America, including the separation of powers among the major branches of government and the establishment of a supreme court. The principles adopted from Canada were federal system of government with strong centre and also distribution of powers between central government and state governments along with placing residuary powers with central government. From Ireland, directive principle of state policy was adopted. From Germany, the principle of suspension of fundamental rights during emergency was adopted. From Australia, the idea of having a Concurrent list of shared powers was used as well and some of the terminology was utilized for the preamble.

Amendments: The process of re-writing any part of the constitution is called amendment. Amendments to the Constitution are made by the Parliament, the procedure for which is laid out in Article 368. An amendment bill must be passed by both the Houses of Parliament by a two-thirds majority and voting. In addition to this, certain amendments which pertain to the federal nature of the Constitution must be ratified by a majority of state legislatures.

As of September 2013 there have been 120 amendment bills presented in the Parliament, out of which 98 have been passed to become Amendment Acts. Most of these amendments address issues dealt with by statute in other democracies. However, the Constitution is so specific in spelling out government powers that many of these issues must be addressed by constitutional amendment. As a result, the document is amended roughly twice a year.

In 2000 the National Commission to Review the Working of the Constitution (NCRWC) was set up to look into updating the constitution.

Salient Features of the Constitution of India

The unique and distinct features of the Constitution of India, as summarized by Dasgupta, 2012, are mentioned as following.

Longest written constitution

Indian Constitution can be called the largest written constitution in the world because of its contents. In its original form, it consisted of 395 Articles and 8 Schedules to which additions have been made through subsequent amendments. At present it contains 448 Articles and 12 Schedules, and more than 80 amendments. There are various factors responsible for the long size of the constitution. One major factor was that the framers of the constitution borrowed provisions from several sources and several other constitutions of the world. Further, a detail list of individual rights, directive principles of state policy and the details of administration procedure were laid down to make the Constitution clear and unambiguous for the ordinary citizen.

Partly Rigid and Partly Flexible

The Constitution of India is neither purely rigid nor purely flexible. There is a harmonious blend of rigidity and flexibility. Some parts of the Constitution can be amended by the ordinary law-making process by Parliament. Certain provisions can be amended, only when a Bill for that purpose is passed in each house of Parliament by a majority of the total membership of that house and. by a majority of not less than two-third of the members of that house present and voting. Then there are certain other provisions which can be amended by the second method described above and are ratified by the legislatures of not less than one-half of the states before being presented to the President for his assent. It must also be noted that the power to initiate bills for amendment lies in Parliament alone, and not in the state legislatures.

A Democratic Republic

India is a democratic republic. It means that sovereignty rests with the people of India. They govern themselves through their representatives elected on the basis of universal adult franchise.

The President of India, the highest official of the state is elected for a fixed term. Although, India is a sovereign republic, yet it continues to be a member of the Commonwealth of Nations with the British Monarch as its head. Her membership of the Commonwealth does not compromise her position as a sovereign republic. The Commonwealth is an association of free and independent nations. The British Monarch is only a symbolic head of that association.

Parliamentary System of Government

India has adopted the Parliamentary system as found in Britain. In this system, the executive is responsible to the legislature, and remains in power only as long as it enjoys the confidence of the legislature. The president of India, who remains in office for five years, is the nominal, titular or constitutional head. The Union Council of Ministers with the Prime Minister as its head is drawn from the legislature. It is collectively responsible to the House of People (Lok Sabha), and has to resign as soon as it loses the confidence of that house. The President shall exercise his powers according to the advice of the Union Council of Ministers, the real executive. In the states too, the government is Parliamentary in nature.

A Federation

Article 1 of the Constitution of India says: - "India that is Bharat shall be a Union of States". Though the word 'Federation' is not used, the government is federal. A state is federal when (a) there are two sets of governments and there is distribution of powers between the two, (b) there is a written constitution, which is the supreme law of the land and (c) there is an independent judiciary to interpret the constitution and settle disputes between the centre and the states. All these features are present in India. There are two sets of government, one at the centre, the other at state level and the distribution of powers between them is quite detailed in our Constitution. The Constitution of India is written and the supreme law of the land. At the apex of single integrated judicial system, stands the Supreme Court which is independent from the control of the executive and the legislature.

But in spite of all these essential features of a federation, Indian Constitution has an unmistakable unitary tendency. While other federations like U.S.A. provide for dual citizenship, the Indian Constitution provides for single citizenship. There is also a single integrated judiciary for the whole country. The provision of All India Services, like the Indian Administrative Service, the India Police Service, and Indian Forest Service prove another unitary feature. Members of these services are recruited by the Union Public Service Commission on an All-India basis. Since these services are controlled by Union Government, to some extent this constitutes a constraint on the autonomy of states.

Fundamental Rights

The constitution of India affirms the basic principle that every individual is entitled to enjoy certain basic rights and part III of the Constitution deals with those rights which are known as fundamental rights. Originally there were seven categories of rights, but now they are six in number. They are (i) Right to equality, (ii) Right to freedom, (iii) Right against exploitation, (iv) Right to freedom of Religion, (v) Cultural and Educational rights and (vi) Right to constitutional remedies. Right to property (Article-31) originally a fundamental right has been omitted by the 44th Amendment Act. 1978. It is now a legal right.

The right to move to the Supreme Court straight for the enforcement of fundamental rights has been guaranteed under Article 32 (Right to Constitutional Remedies).

Directive Principles of State Policy

A novel feature of the Constitution is that it contains a chapter on the Directive Principles of State Policy. These principles are in the nature of directives to the government to implement them for establishing social and economic democracy in the country.

It embodies important principles like adequate means to livelihood, equal pay for both men and women, distribution of wealth so as to subserve the common good, free and compulsory primary education, right to work, public assistance in case of old age, unemployment, sickness and disablement, the organization of village Panchayats, special care to the economically backward sections of the people etc.

Fundamental Duties

A new part IV (A) after the Directive Principles of State Policy was incorporated in the Constitution by the 42nd Amendment, 1976 for fundamental duties. These duties are: (i) To abide by the Constitution and respect its ideals and institutions, the National Flag and the National Anthem; (ii) To cherish and follow the noble ideals, which inspired our national struggle for freedom; (iii) To uphold and protect the sovereignty, unity and integrity of India; (iv) To defend the country and render national service when called upon to do so; (v) to promote harmony and the spirit of common brotherhood amongst all the people of India transcending religious, linguistic, regional or sectional diversities, to renounce practices derogatory to the dignity of women; (vi) to value and preserve the rich heritage of our composite culture; (vii) to protect and improve the natural environments including forests, lakes, rivers and wild life and to have compassion for living creatures; (viii) to develop scientific temper, humanism and the spirit of inquiry and reform; (ix) to safeguard public property and to abjure violence; (x) to strive towards excellence in all spheres of individual and collective activity so that the nation constantly rises to higher levels of endeavour and achievement.

The purpose of incorporating these duties in the Constitution is just to remind the people that while enjoying their right as citizens, should also perform their duties, for rights and duties are correlative.

Secular State

A secular state is neither religious nor irreligious, or anti-religious. Rather it is quite neutral in matters of religion. India being a land of many religions, the founding fathers of the Constitution thought it proper to make it a secular state. India is a secular state, because it makes no discrimination between individuals on the basis of religion. It neither encourages nor discourages any religion. On the contrary, right to freedom of religion is ensured in the Constitution and people belonging to any religious group have the right to profess, practice or propagate any religion they like.

An Independent Judiciary

The judiciary occupies an important place in our Constitution and it is also made independent of the legislature and the executive. The Supreme Court of India stands at the apex of single integrated judicial system. It acts as protector of fundamental rights of Indian citizens and guardian of the Constitution. If any law passed by the legislature or action taken by the executive contravenes the provisions of the Constitution, they can be declared as null and void by the Supreme Court. Thus, it has the power of judicial review. But judicial review in India constitutes a middle path between the American judicial supremacy on the one hand and British Parliamentary supremacy in the other.

Single Citizenship

The Constitution of India recognizes only single citizenship. In the United States, there is provision of dual citizenship. In India, we are citizens of India only, not of the respective states to which we belong. This provision would help in promoting unity and integrity of the nation.

The Enduring Quality of the Constitution of India

The Constitution provided autonomy for the functioning of the three wings of governance, Parliament, the Executive and the Judiciary with a clear demarcation of their respective roles.

Constitutional history in the recent past has witnessed several land mark judgments, some of the significant ones being the Kesavananda Bharati case and the Golaknath case where in the Supreme Court upheld that the basic structure of the Constitution and the Fundamental Rights are beyond the legislative authority of Parliament.

2.4 Striving towards Good Governance: The Indian Experience

Introduction

The processes of growth and economic development in India have had to encounter a parallel exacerbation of inequity and exclusion over regions of the country, sections of the people and sectors of the economy. Bridging the gap, experiences of those excluded, between the availability of, and access to, goods, services and the fruits of development, remain a challenge.

Good Governance: Historical Instances

History records instances of good governance from the epic period of Ramayana and Mahabharata through the ancient (Kautilya's Arthashastra), medieval (Mughal administration) and modern times (British rule).

Kautilya's Arthashastra dealt with the system of administration in the Mauryan Empire. While some aspects of the Arthashastra may have lost relevance today, many remain worthy of emulation. Kautilya stressed on a system which is transparent, responsive, responsible and accountable and these remain the most recognized even now. The idea of today's welfare state, also finds place in the Arthashastra.

In the Mughal Empire, features such as sound maintenance of law, order, peace, and, fair and speedy administration of justice, and emphasis on local governance, were important features.

Governance and administration under the British rule, witnessed a series of experiments, changes and innovations, but retained some of the features of the Mughal period. Perhaps the most significant legally by the British rule that needs specific mention in this context, is the modernized and rationalized structure of the civil service in India.

Constraints of Good Governance- Some Recent Rulings

Though the concept of Good Governance has been around in India from the early days of economic reforms, e-governance, as a means of good governance, is a recent phenomenon. The inception of e-governance has helped decision-makers, administrators, the common man and formal and informal entities in appreciating the essence of good governance. Acknowledging the importance and necessity of e-governance, the Central and State governments have taken several steps to bring different areas under its fold.

A few instances of good governance in India described below illustrate not only the good practices, but also certain constraints which have to be overcome.

Some Practices of Good Governance and their Drawbacks

Quite a few initiatives of practicing good governance, mainly through e-governance, have been observed across states in India. A study by Saxena, 2005, compiles the following, in this regard.

"Andhra Pradesh has computerized its land records down to the sub-registrars' level, reducing the time, corruption and the government's own transaction costs in providing this service. Karnataka's Bhoomi project is another excellent example of how the use of IT in the land records department has actually led to empowerment of farmers...Under the Bhoomi (or 'land') project revenue department has computerized the state's 20 million rural land records, involving some 6.7 million farmers...Municipal authorities in Delhi are using software that enables them to collect property taxes more efficiently. Litigants can now track the progress of their cases in the Supreme Court, and have access to all judgments since 1952 on compact disc. Pondicherry has computerized its ration card system" (Saxena A., 2005).

Now, it becomes very important to understand whether the initiatives have been successful in meeting the desired goals. As assessed in the study by Saxena, 2005, most of the initiatives for good governance have only partially succeeded or resulted in temporary gains have accrued.

For example the Gyandoot project is identified as a model of greater transparency that reduced corruption, it has however been pointed out that it did not meet all its objectives. It has been said that transparency was not fully ensured in the provision of services and coverage of places. There is no denying the fact, however, that the project represents a major stride towards achieving transparency, despite many constraints. Similarly, data sources and data bases were not reliable in the Bhoomi project. Admittedly the project failed to address forged data fed online. The inability of that project to address issues of gender inequality has also been pointed out by Acharya.

Constraints in Practicing Good Governance and Causal Factors

Out of the many states that have undertaken the implementation of good governance through e-governance, only few states viz., Andhra Pradesh, Tamil Nadu and Karnataka, have taken the lead and come out with practices that can be upheld as models. Although other states like West Bengal, Rajasthan, Madhya Pradesh, Maharashtra, Gujarat and Kerala are striving towards achieving the same, but they do have a long way to go; as assessed by NASSCOM. Therefore, it becomes not only important, but necessary to analyze the constraints that are hindering their path of development in good governance.

A major factor causing such inter-state disparities has been identified as the rigidity of the bureaucracy in the Indian administrative system. According to a NASSCOM study, "only 1% of Indian Administration can be computerized or we can say only 1 % of government can be converted to e-government" (Saxena A., 2005). Bureaucracy is not only observed in the structure of system, but also in the mindsets of people. For example, bringing in good governance through e-governance requires re-engineering of the government processes through computerization of all records; this shift from the manual mode of work to a computerized process is not easily accepted, and hence not completely implemented in many cases. As a result, the failure to eliminate and to update earlier work procedures delays decision-making and implementation, result yielding only partial success. Another issue with the existing bureaucratic system is its top-down approach; this excludes the demand side of the people unlike the bottom-up approach. Another major constraint is the lack of infrastructure required for implementing e-governance. Besides the massive requirement of means of connectivity like the internet, etc., continuous supply of adequate power is another major challenge in India.

Good governance is also constrained by factors such as the transfers of officials and changes of political leaders. Implementation is often adversely affected by such changes and, is, unfortunately, inevitable in the extant system.

The difficulty in ensuring an inclusive approach causes the 'digital divide'- sharp variations in access to computer and internet services, which, unless remedied, can lead to widening inequalities in the delivery of goods and services, benefitting the rich and the affluent, and denying the same to the poor and weaker sections.

Prominent among the factors cited above are "lack of access to technology... lack of content in local languages... threat from private entrepreneur-ship model... manner in which IT is being applied in villages... lack of participatory knowledge management system", as pinpointed in a study by Saxena in 2005. Inadequate access to technology is still common in rural and peri-urban India and the urban poor ,Even though rural areas consume many IT products, access is limited by factors such as uncertain power supply, lack of familiarity with the English language, shortage of complementary connectivity tools such as scanners, microphones, etc and is exasperated by many factors including issues relating to caste and gender. Increasing privatization of this sector can also push up the costs of the products and make them more unaffordable to the poor Creation of awareness in rural areas about the availability of goods and services is also a challenge.

Overcoming political reluctance to implementing practices of good governance is a challenge that must be tackled in the future. In the ultimate analysis there is no substitute for strong political will backed by an efficient administration if the benefits of good governance are to reach the public at large. As Gandhiji said "an ounce of practice is worth more than tons of preaching".

2.5 Fund Utilization and Ethics

Fund utilization constitutes an important aspect of public management. In our country, intergovernmental transfers from the centre to the states take place through three channels: statutory and other transfers mandated by the Finance Commission and formula-based transfers for State Plan Schemes from the ministries and organizations of the government of India. Prudent Fund utilization is a major concern from the perspective of their ethical management.

Many lapses can occur in public fund utilization. In a performance audit, by the Comptroller and Auditor General (CAG) it was found that in 14 states, 143 works were abandoned or remained incomplete after spending Rs. 43.85 crore and 149 works costing Rs. 54.71 crore were either abandoned or not taken up in 12 states on account of non-availability of land, want of forest clearance, land disputes or roads were already constructed by other agencies or connectivity was already existing. All of these point to lapses in ethical management. Additionally, that report also indicated that the quality of roads built was shoddy as a result of the absence of proper checks and balances in management and monitoring. The following table reflected the situation:

Table 2.1 Central allocation and release, and utilization of funds under PMGSY during 2008-09 & 2009-10 – Other States

(Rs. In crores)

	2008-09				2009-10			
State	**Alloca-tion**	**Release**	**Expen-diture**	**Percen-tage**	**Alloca-tion**	**Release**	**Expen-duture**	**Percen-tage**
Andhra pradesh	105	471	494	105	90	877	886	101
Bihar	337	1065	1068	100	288	1751	1875	107
Chhattisgarh	240	976	863	88	205	540	805	149
Goa	5	0	0	0	2	0	0	0
Gujarat	65	230	255	111	56	194	190	98
Haryana	30	272	313	115	26	255	277	108
Himachal pradesh	87	269	241	89	74	125	220	176
Jharkhand	175	211	211	100	149	418	458	110
Karnataka	110	640	550	86	94	765	884	116
Kerala	30	84	84	100	26	100	114	114
Madhya Pradesh	440	1895	2198	116	376	2136	2235	105
Maharashtra	145	1030	930	90	124	949	995	105
Orrissa	273	1251	1163	92	233	1594	1895	119
Punjab	35	243	269	111	30	348	323	93
Rajasthan	234	1771	1696	96	201	603	795	132
Tamilnadu	90	89	128	144	77	525	560	107
Uttarpradesh	375	1676	2000	119	324	2845	2915	102
Uttarakhand	100	117	153	131	85	166	173	104
West Bengal	226	635	583	92	193	375	576	154
Total	**3102**	**12925**	**13200**	**102**	**2651**	**14567**	**16175**	**111**

Source: NRRDA, Ministry of Rural Development, Government of India, New Delhi

The same report pointed out that there were obvious discrepancies in terms of fund utilization with many of the disbursements rolled out in the last quarter instead of evenly spreading over the earlier quarters. There were delays in disbursement, as a result of lack of timely audit and a poor accountability.

3. ETHICS IN GOVERNANCE

Good governance must be founded on moral virtues ensuring stability and harmony. Confucius described righteousness as the foundation of good governance and peace. Elimination of corruption is not only a moral imperative but an economic necessity for a nation on the verge of being a superpower. Transparency, Accountability, Efficiency, Equity are few of the basic attributes of Good Governance. Practices like Right to Information, Citizen Charter are a step in the right direction towards achieving Good Governance.

3.1 Corruption

"The foundation of good Governance is righteousness in public affairs. The King his son- including relatives- his ministers and the State employees who have taken the oath of their offices to uphold dharma and to take acre of public needs must not act unjustly or unethically because if they do so, they will not only destroy the moral basis of Governance but will also turn the state into a hell"

- Mahabharata, Shantiparva

Corruption is an abuse of the public resources or public position for private gains. It is a complex concept and occurs both in the developed and developing countries. Public corruption can take place in two manners. In the first case the public officials embezzle the money from the public purse for their own benefit. Public corruption also takes place when the public systems are dysfunctional and citizens are able to get public services only after paying a bribe. This slows down the development process.

Different Types of Corruption

The different types of corruption include bribery, embezzlement, fraud and clientilism and nepotism. These behaviors are prevalent in all the classes of the society. The government sector, private sector and the civil society are all affected by the menace of the corruption.

Bribery: It is the form of the corruption that is most prevalent and receives the greatest share of attention. Bribery refers to the offering, giving, soliciting, or receiving of any item of value as a means of influencing the actions of an individual holding a public or legal duty. This type of action results in matters that should be handled objectively being handled in a manner best suiting the private interests of the decision maker. Bribery in bureaucracy has been viewed as a reason for the higher cost of production of goods and services.

Embezzlement: It is the form of corruption which occurs when the public officials misappropriate public money or government property.

Fraud: It is the form of corruption that occurs when one party cheats the other through deceit. In this type of corruption one party distorts information and manipulates facts for personal profit. Identity theft, forgery, smuggling and counterfeiting are examples of fraud.

Nepotism: It is the form of corruption which occurs when officials favor relatives or friends. This type of favoritism occurs where the officials hold discretionary powers and decision making authority. It occurs in both public and private sectors.

Many Forms of Corruption at different levels have been studied. These include :

Systemic corruption: When corruption is an integrated and essential aspect of the economic, social and political system, embedded in a wider situation that helps sustain it.

Sporadic (individual) corruption: The opposite of systemic corruption, which occurs irregularly. Without threatening the mechanisms of control or the economy, it can seriously undermine morale and sap resources.

Petty Corruption: Small scale, bureaucratic or petty corruption is the everyday corruption that takes place at the implementation end of system, where the lowest rungs of officials deal with the common man.

Corruption: A Menace

In a corrupt society, the decisions are determined by ulterior motives with little or no concern for the public good or the wider community. Every citizen of the country is affected by the corruption directly or indirectly. The effects of corruption include but are not limited to increasing poverty, environmental degradation, increasing costs of goods and services. If the institutional capacity of a nation is weak, then government cannot effectively implement the policies and programs. The economic stability and economic growth of the country are affected by high levels of corruption. The public officials are not able to properly perform their functions because of corruption.

Corruption is one of the major reasons for the poverty of the country. It creates an environment of uncertainty which hampers the economic growth. The government services like health and education are unequally distributed among the citizens. The overall wealth of the country is reduced which discourages the businesses from operating in the area. Due to corruption the elite have the power to influence the implementation of the rules and laws. The poor are the worst affected because of administrative barriers and institutional failures. The trust in the government is broken because of corruption.

Causes of Corruption

A society is prone to corruption when its institutions are weak and the public accountability is minimal. When the institutions of the government are inefficient, secretive and unresponsive, then the government is more vulnerable to corruption.

The specific reasons which act as a catalyst for the promotion of corruption are:

Lack of Transparency creates opportunity for public officials to abuse the office for private gains. When the information is not freely available and accessible to the citizens then they are not able to make the public officials accountable. This lack of transparency and accountability helps corruption to flourish.

Lack of Punitive Measures is a major reason for growth of corruption. Lack of strong enforcement measures allow people in power to indulge in various corrupt activities. Absence of punitive measures for promoting transparency, monitoring and accountability through an independent and powerful judiciary creates an environment where people in power believe they can get away with corruption.

Poverty: Poverty is a major cause of corruption. Statistically, the most corrupt countries in the world are still battling with poverty.

Lack of Decentralization and Lawlessness: Over centralization and excessive monopoly cause the absence of a level playing field. This allows the people having discretionary powers to abuse it. On the other hand where the control of government is weak, people can live safely outside the ambit of the law.

Poor Incentives and Remuneration Structures: Inadequate incentive and remuneration structure force people to supplement their incomes by indulging in corrupt behavior. The lack of a proper incentive structure also takes away the motivation to work hard.

Seven Principles of Public Life

Lord Nolan of UK in his report to parliament has stated seven principles of public life which are:

(i) **Selflessness**: Holders of public office should take decision based only on public interest. They should not act in a manner to gain material or financial benefit for themselves or their family and friends.

(ii) **Integrity**: Holders of public office should not place themselves under any sort of obligation to any organizations or persons which can influence their decision making ability.

(iii) **Objectivity**: Any decision made by the public officials should be based only on merit as the sole criteria.

(iv) **Accountability**: Holders of public office should be accountable for their decisions to public and submit themselves to different types of scrutiny which is appropriate for their office.

(v) **Openness**: Public officials should be as open as possible about all the decisions and actions they take. They should give all the reasons for their decisions.

(vi) **Honesty**: Holders of the public office have a duty to declare any private interests relating to their public duties and to take steps to resolve any conflicts arising in a way that it protects the public interest.

(vii) **Leadership**: The holders of public office should promote and support these principles by leadership and exemplary behavior.

Code of Conduct and Code of Ethics

Ethics is a set of principles of right conduct. It is a set of values which helps guide the actions, behavior and choices. Individuals and organizations both have ethical standards. The ethical standard for an organization ensures that people belonging to an organization have uniformity and consistency in their approach to work.

Ethical Framework for Legislators in Different Countries

Various countries have prescribed a code of ethics for ministers. In Canada the 'Guide for ministers (2006)' sets out core principles regarding the responsibilities of the ministers. This guide includes standards of conduct expected of ministers and addresses a range of administrative, procedural and institutional matters.

In **Great Britain** the ministerial code provides guidance to ministers on how to act and how to perform their duties in order to uphold the ethical standards. Different principles based on past precedents have been listed which may apply in a particular situation. The code rests the responsibility of acting and working according to the principles mentioned in code on individual ministers personally. It says that the ministers have to justify their action and conduct in parliament.

The **United Kingdom** House of Commons adopted its code of conduct in 1995. This code of conduct assists the members in performing their functions and obligations towards the house, the nation and the public and provides guidance on the standard of conduct expected of members in discharging their public and legislative duties.

The **United States** constitution in Article 1, Section 5 grants broad authority to the Congress to discipline its members. In 1968 senate adopted its first official code of conduct. This code of conduct was amended and revised in 1977. The senate code of conduct regulates gifts, financial disclosures, post employment restrictions etc.

Indian Experiences

The Committee on Ethics of the Rajya Sabha, the first such Committee of any legislature in India, was constituted by the Chairman, Rajya Sabha on 4 March 1997 to oversee the moral and ethical conduct of the Members and to examine the cases referred to it with reference to ethical and other misconduct of Members. It was provided that in all respects of procedure and other matters, the rules applicable to the Committee of Privileges shall apply to the Ethics Committee with such variations and modifications as the Chairman, Rajya Sabha may, from time to time, make. The committee was inaugurated by the then Vice-President of India and the Chairman of Rajya Sabha, Shri K.R. Narayanan, on 30 May 1997.

The Committee in its first report dealt with matters like values in public life, electoral reforms and criminalization of politics. A framework was suggested for Code of Conduct of Members of Rajya Sabha.

In the Second Report having laid down a general Framework of Code of Conduct for Members of Rajya Sabha, the Committee felt the need for providing a procedure for enforcing the Code as well as dealing with cases of ethical misconduct by members. In its second report the Committee considered the procedure for making a complaint to the Committee, taking notice suo moto as well as, the mechanism for investigation of a complaint and the question of providing penalties for a proved unethical conduct or for violating the Code.

In the Third Report, the Committee dealt with issues germane to the behavior of Members in House as well as outside of it. The Committee reiterated that a holistic view had to be taken while dealing with the issues relating to decline in standards of behaviour of the members and that ethical questions cannot be dealt with by legislation alone. These are mainly matters of one's conscience.

The fourth report dealt with the discipline and decorum in the Rajya Sabha, Code of Conduct, registration of interest and Committee's power to recommend sanctions.

Existing Framework

The Code of Conduct for Members of Rajya Sabha requires them to acknowledge their responsibility to maintain the public trust reposed in them, to work diligently to discharge their mandate for the common good of the people and to hold in high esteem the Constitution, the Law, Parliamentary Institutions and above all the general public. The code also exhorts them constantly to strive to translate into reality the ideals laid down in the Preamble to the Constitution. The following are the principles the Members are required to abide by in their dealings:

(i) Members must not do anything that brings disrepute to Parliament and affects their credibility.

(ii) Members must utilize their position as Members of Parliament to advance the general well-being of the people.

(iii) In their dealings if Members find that there is a conflict between their personal interests and the public trust which they hold, they should resolve such a conflict in a manner that their private interests are subordinated to the duty of their public office.

(iv) Members should always see that their private financial interests and those of the members of their immediate family do not come in conflict with the public interest and if any such conflict ever arises, they should try to resolve such a conflict in a manner that the public interest is not jeopardised.

(v) Members should never expect or accept any fee, remuneration or benefit for a vote given or not given by them on the floor of the House, for introducing a Bill, for moving a resolution or desisting from moving a resolution, putting a question or abstaining from asking a question or participating in the deliberations of the House or a Parliamentary Committee.

(vi) Members should not take a gift which may interfere with honest and impartial discharge of their official duties. They may, however, accept incidental gifts or inexpensive mementoes and customary hospitality.

(vii) Members holding public offices should use public resources in such a manner as may lead to public good.

(viii) If Members are in possession of a confidential information owing to their being Members of Parliament or Members of Parliamentary Committees, they should not disclose such information for advancing their personal interests.

(ix) Members should desist from giving certificates to individuals and institutions of which they have no personal knowledge and are not based on facts.

(x) Members should not lend ready support to any cause of which they have no or little knowledge.

(xi) Members should not misuse the facilities and amenities made available to them.

(xii) Members should not be disrespectful to any religion and work for the promotion of secular values.

(xiii) Members should keep uppermost in their mind the fundamental duties listed in part IVA of the Constitution.

(xiv) Members are expected to maintain high standards of morality, dignity, decency and values in public life.

Committee of Ethics in the Lok Sabha

There is a Committee of Ethics in Lok Sabha to oversee the Moral and Ethical conduct of the members of the house. In its first report the committee observed that the norms of ethical behavior of members have been adequately provided in Rules of Procedure and Conduct of Business in the Lok Sabha. Apart from the existing norms the committee stated that the legislatures should abide by the following ethical principles:

- Members should utilize their position for the general advancement of the wellbeing of the citizens. Conflict between private interest and Public Interest should be solved in such a manner that the Private interest is subordinated to Public interest.
- Members must maintain high standards of Dignity, Decency and Morality in public life.
- Members using Public Office should use public resources for Public Good. Members must remember their Fundamental duties enlisted in the constitution.

Code of Conduct for Civil Servants

The change in the nature of the State from a regulatory state to a welfare state has also brought a change in the nature of the functions performed by the Civil Servants. The citizens have also become empowered and expect the civil servants to perform their duties impartially and effectively. This has necessitated the need for a code of ethics for the civil servants.

Impartiality, integrity, political neutrality, anonymity etc are the hallmark of an efficient civil service. Different countries have adopted different methods to uphold these principles. In Australia these values have been embodied in laws and provided a legal backing. United Kingdom and New Zealand have established a set of principles to guide civil servants' behavior in terms of legally enforceable code of conduct and setting out standards of behavior expected from Civil Servants.

In India the current set of ethical norms are the conduct Rules contained in the Central Services (Conduct) Rules 1964 and analogous rules applicable to members of All India Services or employees of various state Governments.

3.2 Code of Ethics

The constitution of Ethics Committees in organizations is a primary step towards establishing a code of ethics. Much has been said and written about goals or purposes of public and private sector organisations, the political, social and economic environment within which they operate, their functions, the processes and structures adopted to achieve their objectives, the type of people employed, the skills required and the techniques adopted. However, any debate that relies upon the view that the public sector and the private sector can be treated as homogenous entities will prove, ultimately, to be an unrealistic exercise. Public services are unique in that they are often charged with service delivery mechanisms, and consequently shoulder responsibilities relating to monitoring and regulation. The political and social environment associated with public organizations also contributes uniquely to the modus operandi of public service organizations. Public servants have an added responsibility in having to render services transparently and promptly. Ethics is again important from the perspective of the public sector becoming more responsible in building public confidence.

In this context, Steinberg & Austen have suggested that frustration, turf wars, nepotism, and the need to survive at any cost substantially contribute to unethical behavior on the part of public servants.

Personal values matter to a great degree as far as the implementation of the code of ethics is concerned. Several researchers and philosophers agree with the view that values are central to the domain of morality and that ethical principles are indeed the product of the values in place. Values are considered to be universal because they remain unaltered over cultural and religious differences. According to Mark Schwartz, six moral values form the bedrock for the implementation of codes of ethics, based on a comprehensive review of existing normative research on ethics. These include:

1. Trustworthiness (including notions of honesty, integrity, transparency, reliability, and loyalty);
2. Respect (including notions of respect for human rights);
3. Responsibility (including notions of accountability, excellence, and self-restraint);
4. Fairness (including notions of process, impartiality, and equity);
5. Caring (including the notion of avoiding unnecessary harm); and
6. Citizenship (including notions of obeying laws and protecting the environment).

The important aspect here is to ensure relevance to different practical situations.

Ethics is a transnational concept and cuts across boundaries and cultures. The universality of ethics remains the same whether it is applied in an oriental context or an occidental one, albeit with subtle differences depending on the context. What works in Hong Kong should also work in India or Sweden. Scams such as those associated with organizations such as Enron and Arthur Andersen affected the performance and the survival of their subsidiaries in various locations worldwide.

It should be noted that ethical dilemmas cannot be quantified and their resolution require a careful application of moral and cognitive judgments in order to be resolved. This assumes even more importance when one considers the prevalence of relationship based cultures in Asia, known by different names. China is known for its "Guanxi"system. Simply put, Guanxi is the system of social networks and influential relationships which facilitate business and other dealings. It is therefore, a central and formalized institution and also serves as a mechanism for informal mediation. Guanxi arises from the nature of personalised networks of influence in Chinese society. A very thin line separates Guanxi and other forms of relationships. It also refers to family relationships that have been carefully built and nurtured over years - the central point being a deep rooted trust- a trust placed by parent in child, husband in wife, teacher in student, ruler in subject, etc., in the Chinese context.

In order to counter the conflicts of interest stemming from "Guanxi", Chinese governments have introduced ethical codes that mandate listed companies to specially respect the legal rights of banks and other creditors, employees, consumers, suppliers, the community and other stakeholders. Such a dispensation ensures that the company is involved in the maximization of shareholder benefits, as well as the public interest.

3.3 Lokpal

Corruption is an issue of national concern, especially in the context of India being ranked85thinthe list of 175 countries worldwide on the Corruption Perceptions Index prepared by Transparency International. According to a study by Trace International as cited in a report of the Central Vigilance Commission (CVC) of India some startling facts that stand out as regards the state of bribery and corruption in India are:

- 91% of the bribes were demanded by government officials.
- 77% of the bribes demanded were for avoiding harm rather than to gain any advantage.
- of which 51% were for timely delivery of services to which the individual was already entitled.

The losses on account of corruption are also quite substantial. There are estimates that about 2 lakh crore rupees are lost every year following tax evasion, and about approximately Rs. 40,000 crore rupees per year because of delays in the implementation of projects. Over Rs. 2,00,000 crores ($34,393 million) was reported as the loss suffered by the exchequer during the period 2002 to 2011 on account of illegal financial flows caused by lacunae in implementation.

With a view to strengthening vigilance, containing graft, and preventing harassment of honest civil servants, the institutions of Lokpal at the national level and Lokayukta (at the state level), have been contemplated. The provisions of Lokpal have now been designed to exclude investigation or inquiry into any corruption related allegations made against the Prime Minister as long as the nature of the complaint covers any one of the following:

- Atomic Energy
- Space
- Energy

- Security -Internal and External
- International Relations

However, while the Prime Minister may be investigated on any matter other than the above, the inquiry could be taken up only if atleast two thirds of the Lokpal committee members agree to it.

Further the jurisdiction of the Lokpal is proposed to extend to complaints or grievances made against the following:

- Prime Minister
- Ministers
- Members of the Parliament
- Officers of Groups A,B,C & D or equivalent while serving in the central government
- Officers in bodies which are financed wholly or partly by the government and any officials who or societies which receive more than Rs. 10 lakh in funding from foreign donors.

Institutional Framework for Combating Corruption in India

The Administrative Vigilance Division of the Department of Personnel and Training in the GoI is the nodal agency for dealing with Vigilance and Anti Corruption. Its mandate is to oversee and provide the required directions and insight to the anti corruption program of Government at different levels.

There are other institutions also which are involved at various levels in eradication of Corruption from public services.

The Central Vigilance Commission: The Central Vigilance Commission was established on the recommendation of the Santhanam Committee which is also known as Committee on Prevention of Corruption. Central Vigilance commission was formed in 1964. It was given a statutory status based on the judgment of the Supreme Court of India in Vineet Narain vs. Union of India through the Central Vigilance Commission Act

2003. The Commission exercises superintendence over the working of the Central Bureau of Investigation and the Vigilance administration of the various ministries and the organizations of the Union Government. The CVC advises the union Government on all the matters pertaining to maintenance of the integrity in administration. The Annual Report of the CVC not only gives the details of the work done by it but also brings out the system failures which lead to corruption in various Departments/Organisations, system improvements; various preventive measures and cases in which the Commission's advises were ignored etc.

The CVC is headed by a Central Vigilance Commissioner who is assisted by two Vigilance Commissioners. The Central Vigilance Commission has its own Secretariat, Chief Technical Examiner's Wing (CTE) and a wing of Commissioners for Departmental Inquiries (CDI). As on 21 March 2012, CVC has a staff strength of 257 against sanctioned strength of 299 (including the post of CVC and 2 VCs). The Central Vigilance Commissioner and the Vigilance Commissioners are appointed by the President after obtaining the recommendation of a Committee consisting of:

The Prime Minister – Chairperson

The Home Minister – Member

The Leader of the Opposition in the Lok Sabha – Member

The Central Vigilance Commissioner or any Vigilance Commissioner can be removed from his office only by an order of the President on the ground of proved misbehavior or incapacity after the Supreme Court, on a reference made to it by the President, has, on inquiry, reported that the Central Vigilance Commissioner or any Vigilance Commissioner, as the case may be, ought to be removed.

Vigilance Units in The Government of India: All ministries/ Departments in the Union Government have a Chief Vigilance

Officer who heads the Vigilance division of the organisation concerned advising and assisting the secretary or the head of department in the matters of vigilance. He acts as a link between his concerned department and the Central Vigilance Commission and Central Bureau of Investigation. The different functions performed by the CVO include but is not limited to intelligence gathering about the corrupt practices of the employees of the organisation, investigation of the different complaints received by him, referring matters to the Central Vigilance Commission whenever necessary and asking for their advice on different matters.

Central Bureau of Investigation: It is the prime investigation agency of the Union Government in the anti corruption matters. The CBI was established in 1941 as the Special Police Establishment, tasked with domestic security. It was renamed the Central Bureau of Investigation on 1 April 1963. It derives its mandate from the Delhi Special Police Establishment Act to investigate the different acts of offences pertaining to the corruption and other malpractices involving public servants. Agency headquarters is in the Indian capital, New Delhi, with field offices located in major cities throughout India (including Mumbai). The CBI is overseen by the Department of Personnel and Training of the Ministry of Personnel, Public Grievances and Pensions of the Union Government, headed by a Union Minister who reports directly to the Prime Minister.

According to the CVC Act 2003, a committee recommends a panel of officers for appointment to the post of director of the CBI. It consists of:

Chief Vigilance Commissioner - chairperson

Vigilance Commissioners - members

Secretary, Home Ministry - member

Secretary (Coordination and Public Grievances) in the Cabinet Secretariat - member

When making recommendations, the committee considers the views of the outgoing Director. Final selection is made by the Appointments Committee of the Cabinet from the panel recommended by the selection committee. Central Bureau of Investigation has three units:

(i) Anti Corruption Division
(ii) Economic Offences Wing
(iii) Special Crime Division.

Ombudsman: An ombudsman or public advocate is usually appointed by the government or by parliament, but with a significant degree of independence, who is charged with representing the interests of the public by investigating and addressing complaints of maladministration or violation of rights. Below the national level an ombudsman may be appointed by a state, local or municipal government, and unofficial ombudsmen may be appointed by, or even work for, a corporation such as a utility supplier or a newspaper, for an NGO, or for a professional regulatory body.

Whether appointed by the legislature, the executive, or an organization (or, less frequently, elected by the constituency that he or she serves), the typical duties of an ombudsman are to investigate complaints and attempt to resolve them, usually through recommendations (binding or not) or mediation. Ombudsmen sometimes also aim to identify systemic issues leading to poor service or breaches of people's rights. At the national level, most ombudsmen have a wide mandate to deal with the entire public sector, and sometimes also elements of the private sector (for example, contracted service providers). In some cases, there is a more restricted mandate, for example with particular sectors of society. More recent developments have included the creation of specialized Children's Ombudsman and Information Commissioner Agencies. In general, an ombudsman is a state official appointed to provide a check on government activity in the interests of the citizens, and to oversee the investigation of complaints of improper government activity against the citizen. If the ombudsman finds a complaint to be substantiated, the problem may get rectified, or an ombudsman report is published making recommendations for change.

International Experiences

The first prototype of ombudsmen may have flourished in China during the Qin Dynasty (221 BC), and in Korea during the Joseon Dynasty. The position of Secret royal inspector, or Amhaeng-eosa was unique to the Joseon Dynasty (14th Century AD), where an undercover official directly appointed by the king was sent to local provinces to monitor government officials and look after the populace while travelling incognito. The Roman Tribune had some similar roles, with power to veto acts that infringed upon the Plebeians. Another precursor to the ombudsman was the Turkish Diwan-al-Mazalim which appears to go back to the second Caliph, Umar (634–644) and the concept of Qadi al-Qadat.

An indigenous Swedish, Danish and Norwegian term, Ombudsman is etymologically rooted in the Old Norse word umboðsmaðr, essentially meaning "representative". The modern use of the term began in Sweden, with the Swedish Parliamentary Ombudsman instituted by the Instrument of Government of 1809, to safeguard the rights of citizens by establishing a supervisory agency independent of the executive branch. The predecessor of the Swedish Parliamentary Ombudsman was the Office of Supreme Ombudsman ("Högste Ombudsmannen"), which was established by the Swedish King, Charles XII, in 1713. Charles XII was in exile in Turkey and needed a representative in Sweden to ensure that judges and civil servants acted in accordance with the laws and with their duties. If they did not do so, the Supreme Ombudsman had the right to prosecute them for negligence. In

1719 the Swedish Office of Supreme Ombudsman became the Chancellor of Justice. The Parliamentary Ombudsman was established in 1809 by the Swedish Riksdag, as a parallel institution to the still-present Chancellor of Justice, reflecting the concept of separation of powers as developed by Montesquieu. The Parliamentary Ombudsman is the institution that the Scandinavian countries developed into its contemporary form, and which subsequently has been adopted in many other parts of the world.

Lokpal Bill

The word 'lokpal' was coined by Dr L. M. Singhvi in 1963. It means Legal Representative in India. The concept of a constitutional ombudsman was first proposed in parliament by Law Minister Ashoke Kumar Sen in the early 1960s. In the report on the "Problem of Redress of Citizens Grievances" submitted in 1966 the Administrative Reform Commission recommended the setting up of the institute of Lokpal. The first Jan Lokpal Bill was proposed by Shanti Bhushan in 1968 and passed in the 4th Lok Sabha in 1969, but did not pass through the Rajya Sabha. Subsequently, 'lokpal bills' were introduced in 1971, 1977, 1985, again by Ashoke Kumar Sen, while serving as Law Minister in the Rajiv Gandhi cabinet, and again in 1989, 1996, 1998, 2001, 2005 and in 2008, yet they were never passed. Fifty two years after its first introduction, the Lokpal Bill was finally enacted in India on 18 December 2013.

The Lokpal Bill was, for the first time, presented during the fourth Lok Sabha in 1968, and was passed there in 1969. However, while it was pending in the Rajya Sabha, the Lok Sabha was dissolved, and thus the bill was not passed.

The bill was revived several times in subsequent years, including in 2011. Each time, after the bill was introduced to the House, it was referred to a committee for improvements, to a joint committee of parliament, or to a departmental standing committee of the Home Ministry. Before the government could take a final stand on the issue, the house was dissolved again.

The massive public protest under the leadership of Anna Hazare and his associates played a major role in the passage of the bill in parliament. The campaign began in January 2011 in the backdrop of the several mega scams that surfaced in 2010 like the Commonwealth Sports scam and the telecom spectrum allocation. The movement reached its acme with the Anna Hazare fast at Jantar Mantar which finally set the ball rolling for the Lokpal bill to be passed.

The Present bill was tabled in the Lok Sabha on 22 December 2011 and was passed by the house on 27 December 2011 as The Lokpal and Lokayuktas Bill, 2011. The bill was subsequently tabled in the Rajya Sabha on 29 December 2011. After a marathon debate that stretched until midnight of the following day, the vote failed to take place for lack of time. On 21 May 2012, the bill was referred to a Select Committee of the Rajya Sabha for consideration. The bill was passed in the Rajya Sabha on 17 December 2013 after making certain amendments to the earlier Bill and in the Lok Sabha on 18 December 2013. The Bill received assent from President Pranab Mukherjee on 1 January 2014.

Lokpal and Lokayuktas Bill, 2013

The historic Lokpal and Lokayuktas Bill, 2013 was passed by Indian Parliament paving the way for establishment of a LOKPAL (Ombudsman) to fight corruption in public offices and ensure accountability on the part of public officials, including the Prime Minister, with some safeguards.

Lokpal will consist of a chairperson and a maximum of eight members, of which 50% will be judicial members, 50% members of Lokpal shall be from SC/ST/OBCs, minorities and women Selection of chairperson and members of Lokpal through a selection committee consisting of PM, Speaker of Lok Sabha, leader of opposition in Lok Sabha, Chief Justice of India or a sitting Supreme Court judge nominated by CJI, Eminent jurist to be nominated by President of India on the basis of recommendations of the first four members of the selection committee "through consensus". Lokpal's jurisdiction will cover all categories of public servants. All entities (NGOs) receiving donations from foreign source in the context of the Foreign Contribution Regulation Act (FCRA) in excess of Rs 10 lakh per year will be under the jurisdiction of Lokpal. Lokpal will have power of superintendence and direction over any central investigation agency including CBI for cases referred to them by the ombudsman. Different state governments have to set up the institution of Lokayukt in their states within 365 days after the enactment of act. The main features of the act are:-

A high-powered committee chaired by the PM will recommend selection of CBI director. The collegium will comprise PM, leader of opposition in Lok Sabha and Chief Justice of India. PM has been brought under purview of the Lokpal, so also central ministers and senior officials. Directorate of prosecution will be under overall control of CBI director. At present, it comes under law ministry. Appointment of director of prosecution is to be based on recommendation of the Central Vigilance Commission. Director of prosecution will also have a fixed tenure of two years like CBI chief. Transfer of CBI officers investigating cases referred by Lokpal with the approval of watchdog. Bill incorporates provisions for attachment and confiscation of property acquired by corrupt means, even while prosecution is pending. Bill lays down clear timelines for preliminary enquiry and investigation and trial. Public servants will not present their view before preliminary enquiry if the case requires 'element of surprise' like raids and searches. Bill grants powers to Lokpal to sanction prosecution against public servants.

Legal Framework to Fight Corruption in India

During the Colonial era the Indian Penal Code (IPC) was the main tool to combat corruption in the Public life. The code had a charter on "Offences by Public Servants". Sections 161 to section 165 provided the legal framework to fight corruption and prosecute corrupt public officials. In those days a need for a special law to deal with corruption was not felt. During the Second World War the citizens of the country were facing different hardships as an effect of war and there was an acute shortage of goods which acted as an opportunity for large scale corruption. The trend continued even after the war. The law makers understood the gravity of the situation and in 1947 Prevention of Corruption Act was enacted to fight the menace of bribery and corruption.

The Prevention of Corruption Act 1947: Although the act did not modify or expand the definition of the offences considered as corruption as existing in the IPC but it added a new offence known as "Criminal Misconduct in discharge of duty". To prevent the harassment of the honest officers the act mandated that no court would take the cognizance of offences punishable under the sections161, 164 and 165 without the permission of the competent authority to deal with the public servant.

Criminal Law (Amendment) Act 1952: The amendment brought certain changes in the laws relating to corruption. The quantum of punishment in certain cases was increased and it was also stipulated that all corruption related offences were to be tried by special judges.

Major amendments were carried in the Anti- corruption laws in 1964. The definition of the Public Servant under the IPC was expanded. A provision for the "*in-Camera*" Trials was provided if asked for by either party on trial or desired by the court. The definition of Criminal Misconduct was also expanded. Police officers competent to investigate cases under the act were empowered to inspect bankers' records if they had a reason to suspect any offence committed under the act.

The Prevention of Corruption Act 1988: It consolidates the provisions of the Prevention of Corruption act 1947 and Criminal Law amendment act 1952 and tries to effectively combat corruption in public service. The thrust of the act is on consideration and gratification of all kinds.

Who Guards the Guards?

Quis custodiet ipsos custodes? is a Latin phrase traditionally attributed to the Roman poet Juvenal from his *Satires* which is literally translated as "Who will guard the guards themselves?"

External regulation creates its own complications, bringing with it the complications of supervising the conduct of the mechanisms put in place. In the ultimate analysis that regulation is best which is self imposed. The recent creation of regulators in the fields of banking, insurance, power, telecommunications etc., are examples of external regulations while the Bar Council of India or the Indian Medical Council are in the model of self regulation. Time alone will tell which the best method is.

3.4 Citizens' Charters

It has been recognized world over that good governance is essential for sustainable development, both economic and social. The three essential aspects emphasized in good governance are transparency, accountability and responsiveness of the administration. "Citizens' Charters" initiative is a response to the quest for solving the problems which a citizen encounters, day in and day out, while dealing with the organisations providing public services.

Citizens' Charters as a concept tries to solve the problems that a citizen encounters in dealing with the government organizations. It tries to increase the trust between the Government as service providers and the Citizens as the users.

The concept was first articulated and implemented in United Kingdom in 1991 by the Government headed by John Major as an initiative to continuously improve the quality of service delivery for the citizens and to meet their expectations in terms of quality and other parameters.

It is a document which represents a systematic effort to focus on the commitment of the Government departments, organisation towards citizens in respects of Standard of Services, Information, Choice and Consultation, Non-discrimination and Accessibility, Grievance Redress, Courtesy and Value for Money. This also includes expectations of the Organisation from the Citizen for fulfilling the commitment of the Organisation. All the public services are being funded by the tax payers directly or indirectly so it is the right of the citizens to expect a certain standard of the service and the obligation of the Public servants to provide that standard. Citizens' charters also aim to change the mindset of the public official from that of someone with arbitrary power to someone with a sense of duty and performance and a feeling of obligation towards public. The Citizens' Charter is not legally enforceable and, therefore, is non-justiciable. However, it is a tool for facilitating the delivery of services to citizens with specified standards, quality and time frame etc. with commitments from the Organisation and its clients. Citizens'charter aims to achieve following objectives if successfully implemented.

Increased responsiveness of officials towards the Public improves service delivery resulting in greater public satisfaction with the services. The basic objective of the Citizens' Charter is to empower the citizen in relation to public service delivery. The six principles of the Citizens' Charter movement as originally framed were:

(i) Quality: Improving the quality of services;
(ii) Choice: Providing choice wherever possible;
(iii) Standards: Specify what to expect and how to act if standards are not met;
(iv) Value: Add value for the taxpayers' money;
(v) Accountability: Be accountable to individuals and organisations; and
(vi) Transparency: Ensure transparency in Rules/Procedures/ Schemes/Grievances.

The International Picture

The UK's Citizens' Charter initiative aroused considerable interest around the world and several countries implemented similar programmes e.g., Australia (Service Charter, 1997), Belgium (Public Service Users' Charter 1992), Canada (Service Standards Initiative, 1995), France (Service Charter, 1992), India (Citizens' Charter, 1997), Jamaica (Citizens' Charter 1994), Malaysia (Client Citizens' Charters - A Handbook Charter 2, 1993), Portugal (The Quality Charter in Public Services, 1993), and Spain (The Quality Observatory, 1992) (OECD, 1996).

Some of these initiatives are very similar to the UK model, while others chart new ground by leaning on the service quality paradigm of the Total Quality Management (TQM) movement. Other initiatives are pitched somewhere in between. Even in the UK, in the context of the Next Steps/Modernising Government Initiatives, Citizens' Charters have acquired a service quality face for delivery of public services. The quality tools adopted for improving public services include the Business Excellence Model, Investors in People, Charter Mark, ISO 9000 and Best Value (Government of UK, 1999).

The Government of Malaysia issued Guidelines on the Client's Charter in 1993 to assist government agencies to prepare and implement Client's Charter, which is "a written commitment by an agency to deliver outputs or services according to specified standards of quality" (Government of Malaysia, 1998). A Best Client's Charter Award was instituted in 1993. The Malaysian system of Client's Charter closely follows the UK Model. A distinction is made between agency-wide and unit charters. The concept of 'service recovery' enjoins taking steps to restore the trust and confidence of the client in a proactive manner when things go wrong.

The Commonwealth Government of Australia launched its Service Charter initiative in 1997 as part of its on-going commitment to improve the quality of service provided by agencies to the Australian community by moving the government organisations away from bureaucratic processes to customer-focused outcomes. Service Charters are considered a powerful tool for fostering change and require the organisations to focus on services delivered, to measure and assess performance, and to initiate performance improvement. By providing goals for agencies to strive towards, a Charter acts as a surrogate for competition, where none exists (Department of Finance and Administration, 1999). Centre link is a one-stop shop that provides access to Australian government services for over six million customers. Centre link has adopted one-to-one service as an innovative and personalized approach to service delivery. One-to-one service treats customers with respect and consistency and takes the complexity out of dealing with government.

The Treasury Board of Canada Secretariat started a Service Standard Initiative in 1995 which took its cue from the Citizens' Charters of the United Kingdom, but enlarged the scope considerably. This Service Standard Initiative in Canada was started against the backdrop of citizen expectations relating to friendly, respectful and courteous service, faster response times, extended hours at government offices, and "one-stop-shopping". At the same time there was a need to reduce the deficit and provide value for money through more efficient use of resources (Treasury Board of Canada, 1995).

A comparison of these four major Citizens' Charter initiatives shows that the service quality approach is embedded in them in different degrees and modes. Once a decision is taken to make public services citizen-centric, the customer focus of the Total Quality Management (TQM) variety cannot be far behind. In fact, the Citizens' Charter approach has several things in common with TQM. Both begin by Citizens' Charters - A Hand book focusing on meeting customer/citizen requirements. Other key common elements are conformance to standards, stakeholder involvement and continuous improvement.

Over the years, in India, significant progress has been made in the field of economic development. This, along with a substantial increase in the literacy rate, (from 51.63% to 65.38% in the last decade) has made Indian citizens increasingly aware of their rights. Citizens have become more articulate and expect the administration not merely to respond to their demands but also to anticipate them. It was in this climate that since 1996 a consensus had evolved in the Government on effective and responsive administration. In a Conference of Chief Ministers of various States and Union Territories held on 24 May, 1997 in New Delhi, presided over by the Prime Minister of India, an "Action Plan for Effective and Responsive Government" at the Centre and State levels was adopted. One of the major decisions at that Conference was that the Central and State Governments would formulate Citizens' Charters, starting with those sectors that have a large public interface (e.g., Railways, Telecom, Posts, Public Distribution Systems). These Charters were required to include standards of service and time limits that the public can reasonably expect, avenues of grievance redress and a provision for independent scrutiny with the involvement of citizen and consumer groups. Department of Administrative Reforms and Public Grievances in Government of India (DARPG) initiated the task of coordinating, formulating and operationalizing Citizens' Charters. Guidelines for formulating the Charters as well as a list of do's and don'ts were communicated to various government departments/ organisations to enable them to bring out focused and effective charters. For the formulation of the Charters, the government agencies at the Centre and State levels were advised to constitute a task force with representation from users, senior management and the cutting edge staff. The Charters are expected to incorporate the following elements:-

(i) Vision and Mission Statement;

(ii) Details of business transacted by the organisation;

(iii) Details of clients;

(iv) Details of services provided to each client group;

(v) Details of grievance redress mechanism and how to access it; and

(vi) Expectations from the clients.

Primarily an adaptation of the UK model, the Indian Citizens' Charter has an additional component of 'expectations from the clients' or in other words 'obligations of the users'. Involvement of consumer organisations, citizen groups, and other stakeholders in the formulation of the Citizens' Charter is emphasized to ensure that the Citizens' Charter meets the needs of the users. Regular monitoring, review and evaluation of the Charters, both internally and through external agencies, are enjoined. As on March, 2005, 107 Citizen' Charters had been formulated by the Central Government Ministries/Departments/Organisations and 629 Charters by various agencies of State Governments & Administrations of Union Territories. Most of the national Charters are posted on the government's websites and are open to public scrutiny.

Exemplary implementation of the Citizens' Charter

While the overall efforts and initiatives of the government on Citizens' Charter were continuing, it was realised that exemplary implementation of the Charter in major public interface area of government would not only establish the new concept but also act as a role model for replication in other sectors/areas. The banking sector was identified for this purpose keeping in view the second phase of economic reforms and the fact that this sector was fairly advanced in terms of customer service and was also taking advantage of information technology to speed up various processes. The primary objective of this exercise was to build the Banking Sector as a model of excellence in the implementation of the Citizens' Charter. To begin with, three major National level Banks, namely, Punjab National Bank, Punjab and Sind Bank and Oriental Bank of Commerce, were selected for a Hand-Holding exercise by the DARPG in the year 2000. The following key issues were highlighted for exemplary implementation of the Citizens' Charter:-

(i) Stakeholder involvement in the formulation of Citizens' Charters;

(ii) Deployment of the Citizens' Charters in the Banks by full involvement of the staff, specially the employees at the cutting-edge level;

(iii) Creation of awareness about the Charter amongst the customers of the Banks; and

(iv) Special training for employees at all levels about the concept and implementation of Citizens' Charter.

After an evaluation of the current status of the Charters by the identified banks through independent agencies, Action Plans were chalked out to rectify shortcomings. The Charters were, accordingly, revised and standardized on the basis of the model/ mother Charter developed by the Indian Banks Association (IBA). Training for employees of selected branches through master trainers, trained by the National Institute of Bank Management using a module developed in consultation with Department of ARPG was organised. Several measures to give wide publicity to Citizens' Charter were also undertaken.

Evaluation of Citizens' Charters

An evaluation of the Citizens' Charters of various government agencies was carried out by DARPG and Consumer Coordination Council, New Delhi, an NGO, in October 1998. The results were quite encouraging given the nascent stage of this initiative in India. A brief questionnaire has been circulated to all Ministries/ Departments and State Governments/Union Territories to enable them to undertake an in-house evaluation of their Citizens' Charters. Organisations have also been advised to undertake external evaluations, preferably through NGOs.

During the Year 2002-03, DARPG engaged a professional agency to develop a standardized model for internal and external evaluation of Citizens' Charters in a more effective, quantifiable and objective manner. This agency also carried out evaluation of implementation of Charters in 5 Central Government

Organisations and 15 Departments/Organisations of States of Andhra Pradesh, Maharashtra and Uttar Pradesh.

This Agency was also required to suggest methods for increasing awareness, both within the organisation and among the users, and to suggest possible methods for orientation of management and the staff in the task of formulating and deploying Charters. As per the report of evaluation carried out by the Agency, major findings were:

(i) In majority of cases Charters were not formulated through a consultative process;

(ii) By and large service providers are not familiar with the philosophy, goals and main features of the Charter;

(iii) Adequate publicity to the Charters had not been given in any of the Departments evaluated. In most Departments, the Charters are only in the early stages of implementation;

(iv) No funds have been specifically earmarked for awareness generation of Citizens' Charter or for orientation of staff on various components of the Charter.

Key recommendations, inter alia, include need for citizens and staff to be consulted at every stage of formulation of the Charter, orientation of staff about the salient features and goals/objectives of the Charter; vision and mission statement of the department; and skills such as team building, problem solving, handling of grievances and communication skills, need for creation of database on consumer grievances and redress, need for wider publicity of the Charter through print media, posters, banners, leaflets, handbills, brochures, local newspapers etc., and also through electronic media, earmarking of specific budgets for awareness generation and orientation of staff, and replication of best practices in this field.

Problems in Implementation of Charters

As pointed out, the Citizens' Charters initiative in India had started in 1997 and the Charters formulated are in a nascent stage of implementation. Introduction of a new concept is always difficult in any organisation. Introduction and implementation of the concept of Citizens' Charter in the Government of India was much more difficult due to rules and regulations and lengthy procedures and the rigid attitudes of the work force. The major obstacles encountered in this initiative were:-

(i) The general perception of organisations which formulated Citizens' Charters was that the exercise was to be carried out because there was a direction from the top. The consultation process was minimal or largely absent. It, thus, became one of the routine activities of the organisation and had no focus.

(ii) For any Charter to succeed the employees responsible for its implementation should have proper training and orientation, as commitments of the Charter cannot be expected to be delivered by a work force that is unaware of the spirit and content of the Charter. However, in many cases, the concerned staff were not adequately trained and sensitized.

(iii) Sometimes, transfers and reshuffles of concerned officers at the crucial stages of formulation/ implementation of a Citizens' Charter in an organisation severely undermined the strategic processes which were put in place and hampered the progress of the initiative.

(iv) Awareness campaigns to educate clients about the Charter were not conducted systematically.

(v) In some cases, the standards/time norms of services mentioned in Citizens' Charter were either too lax or too tight and were, therefore, unrealistic and created an unfavorable impression on the clients of the Charter.

(vi) The concept behind the Citizens' Charter was not properly understood.

3.5 Right to Information (RTI)

The RTI Act covers governments at the central, state and the local levels including all bodies owned, controlled or substantially financed and non-government organisation substantially financed directly or indirectly from funds provided by the appropriate government in addition to the executive, judiciary and the legislature. The RTI Act also covers information relating to private bodies which can be accessed under any other law for the time being in force (2(f))

The RTI exempts the following information:

(a) Affecting sovereignty, integrity, security, strategic, scientific or economic, or other interests of the State, relation with foreign state or leading to incitement of an offence;

(b) Forbidden by courts;

(c) Affecting privileges of Parliament or Legislature;

(d) Commercial confidence, trade secrets or intellectual property, unless larger public interest so warrants;

(e) received in confidence from foreign government;

(f) endangers life or physical safety or identifies confidential source of information or assistance

(g) impedes the process of investigation or apprehension

(h) cabinet papers, till after the decision has been taken, and the matter is complete, or over:

(i) personal information which would cause invasion of the privacy unless larger public interest justifies it.

(j) Infringes copyright, except of the state.

(k) Intelligence and security agencies exempt - except for corruption and human rights violation charges

(l) Warranting notice to third party

(m) Most exempt information released after 20 years.

(n) Notwithstanding anything a public authority may allow access to information, if public interests in disclosure outweighs the harm to the protected interests.

Appeals & Penalties against the RTI Act

Appeals and penalties can be made under the purview of the RTI Act. The appeals include First appeal with senior in the department and a Second appeal with Information Commission with the provision that they be settled in 30 to 45 days

Penalties for unreasonable delay are levied at the rate of Rs 250 per day up to Rs 25,000 and for illegitimate refusal to accept application, malafide denial, knowingly providing false information, destruction of information, etc. - up to Rs. 25,000

Responsibilities of the Public Officials

Additionally, the public officials are also required to publish all relevant facts while formulating important policies or announcing the decisions which affect public (4(1)(c)), and for Providing reasons for its administrative or quasi judicial decisions to affected persons (4(1)(d)), providing a large amount of information suomoto (4(2)), and providing information to Information Commission (25(2)).

RTI becomes an important tool from an ethics standpoint because at times, particularly in theIndian context, because of the perceptible high corruption index in the country; and also because of behavioural variables such as the inherent reluctance to acknowledge the presence of corruption despite the widespread prevalence of it. The RTI act has been assumed to be an efficient mechanism in purging away inefficiency and corruption from government, while at the same time allow for increasing the political influence of marginalized citizens.RTI has been successful since its launch in 2005. About two million requests for information under the RTI Act have been filed in the first two and half years after its launch. Many of these requests deal with the nature of corruption by public servants. Researchers also note that they have still not been able to achieve the desired levels of transformation in the country. It is not free from challenges. Research suggests that the success of the RTI has been limited by factors such as:

- uneven public awareness
- poor planning by public authorities and
- bureaucratic indifference or hostility

Free flow of information is a basic human right. Information driven society leads to better transparency and accountability. Openness promotes trials and eliminates errors. Secrecy fosters corruption. The government has to get permission from citizens for everything it does, not the other way round. A free flow of information empowers the citizens to ask questions, know about the working of the government and question the decisions.

Evolution

Transparency in government is not a new issue. John Adams, 2nd president of the United States, wrote, "Liberty cannot be preserved without a general knowledge among the people, who have a right and a desire to know". In other words, a healthy system of government is an open government that allows all who desire to know to find the information they are seeking. Chinese emperors were expected to admit their own imperfection as a proof of their love for the truth and in fear of ignorance and darkness.

Freedom of the Press Act, 1766 in Sweden - Abolished political censorship and provided access for the public to government documents.

UN General Assembly-1946 - first session.

"Freedom of information is a fundamental human right... and the touchstone of all the freedoms to which the UN is consecrated." - Resolution 59 (1)

Universal Declaration of Human Rights, 1948.

"Freedom of expression including Freedom of information and Free Press is a fundamental human right". - Art. 19

The International Covenant on Civil and Political Rights

"Everyone shall have the right to freedom of expression; this right shall include freedom to seek, receive and impart information and ideas of all kinds, regardless of frontiers, either orally, in writing or in print, in the form of art, or through any other media of his choice". - Art. 19 (2)

The Freedom of Information Act, 1966 – The USA.

Offshoot of the activism of newspaper editors: The book "The People's Right to Know" by Harold Cross (a lawyer) became bible for the movement on freedom of information.

COUNTRY	YEAR OF PASSAGE
SWEDEN	1766
COLUMBIA	1888
USA	1966
DENMARK	1970
FRANCE	1978
CANADA	1983

The Indian Story

(i) Bennett Coleman Vs. Union of India, 1973

The Supreme Court ruled that the right to freedom of speech and expression guaranteed under Art. 19 (1) (a) of our Constitution included the right to information.

(ii) State of UP Vs. Raj Narain, 1975

Justice Mathew explicitly stated that it is not in the interest of the public to "cover with a veil of secrecy the common routine business... the responsibility of officials to explain and to justify their acts is the chief safeguard against oppression and corruption".

(iii) S.P. Gupta Vs. Union of India, 1982

The right of the people to know about every public act, and the details of every public transaction undertaken by public functionaries was illustrated.

(iv) People's Union for Civil Liberties Vs. Union of India, 2004

The right to information was further elevated to the status of a human right, necessary for making governance transparent and accountable.

STATE	YEAR OF PASSAGE
Tamil Nadu, Goa	1997
Rajasthan, Karnataka	2000
Delhi	2001
Maharashtra	2002
Madhya Pradesh	2003
Jammu and Kashmir	2004

Towards the RTI ACT

Freedom of Information Bill, 2000 - Passed in the Lok Sabha in July 2000.

Freedom of Information Act, 2002 - Passed by the Parliament but could not be enforced.

Right to Information Act, 2005

The Right to Information Act (RTI) is an Act of the Parliament of India "to provide for setting out the practical regime of right to information for citizens" and replaces the erstwhile Freedom of Information Act, 2002. The Act applies to all States and Union Territories of India except the State of Jammu and Kashmir. Under the provisions of the Act, any citizen may request information from a "public authority" (a body of Government or "instrumentality of State") which is required to reply expeditiously within thirty days. The Act also requires every public authority to computerize their records for wide dissemination and to proactively publish certain categories of information so that the citizens need minimum recourse to request for information formally. This law was passed by Parliament on 15 June 2005 and came fully into force on 13 October 2005.

Private bodies are not within the Act's ambit directly. In a landmark decision of Sarbajit Roy versus Delhi Electricity Regulatory Commission, the Central Information Commission also reaffirmed that privatized public utility companies continue to be within the RTI Act- their privatization not withstanding.

Central Intelligence and Security agencies specified in the Second Schedule like IB, Directorate General of Income tax (Investigation), RAW, Central Bureau of Investigation (CBI), Directorate of Revenue Intelligence, Central Economic Intelligence Bureau, Directorate of Enforcement, Narcotics Control Bureau, Aviation Research Centre, Special Frontier Force, BSF, CRPF, ITBP, CISF, NSG, Assam Rifles, Special Service Bureau, Special Branch (CID), Andaman and Nicobar, The Crime Branch-CID-CB, Dadra and Nagar Haveli and Special Branch, Lakshadweep Police and agencies specified by the State Governments through a Notification will also be excluded. The exclusion, however, is not absolute and these organizations have an obligation to provide information pertaining to allegations of corruption and human rights violations. Further, information relating to allegations of human rights violation could be given but only with the approval of the Central or State Information Commission.

The Central Information Commission (CIC) has held that the political parties are public authorities and answerable to citizens under RTI Act. The CIC, a quasi-judicial body, has said that six national parties: Congress, BJP, NCP, CPI(M), CPI and BSP have been substantially funded indirectly by the Central Government and they have the character of public authority under the RTI Act as they perform public functions. On 12 August 2013, the Congress Party tabled RTI Amendment Bill 2013 in Lok Sabha to keep political parties out of RTI ambit.

Challenges Faced in implementation of the RTI Act

Lack of Awareness: In order to harness the immense potential of Right to information it is very necessary that proper awareness be created among the public regarding the act. People are still not aware of the procedures of the law. The government should hold awareness programs for the general Public.

Pro Active Disclosure: All the public authorities are duty bound to disseminate information prescribed through various means of communications like notice board, news papers, media broadcasts etc., but only very limited number of authorities have done this.

Problems of Delay: Though it is mandatory on the part of the Commission to levy a penalty in case of delay in furnishing information but this practice is seldom followed.

Poor Quality of Information provided: Citizens are often dissatisfied with the quality of information provided.

3.6 Options and Priorities- the Wood or the Tree Dilemma!

Every situation in administration at any level presents options and priorities. To understand the wide gamut of governance issues that one may face, let us look at a hypothetical example. If one were to take over as Prime Minister say two months later, one may face a fiscal crisis, food and nutrition crisis, there may be problems with the welfare of women and children or the environment, there could be issues with neighboring countries, the need to decide whether we bid for the Asian Games, diplomatic parlays may be required to lobby for a place in the Security Council of the United Nations, apart from the usual issues like provision of housing, drinking water or roads, etc. Similarly taking over any job in the government, at the State, or the Centre, in a Public Sector Undertaking or district brings with it its own set of governance issues that present a set of many options for the officer. Of course a lot depends upon what functions your charge covers and you choose to awaken yourself to the issues.

ABC, VED and Twin-Track Governance

The important thing to remember here is that, while taking up a new assignment, it is much more important to find the right questions to ask. Answers will come on their own in due course.

1. Draw up a list of things to be done
2. First choose from your list, Category A - things which you want to achieve during your tenure
3. Choose a Category C: things that you want to do away with, a negative list if you wish- such as combating corruption or downsizing staff in excess of the requirement or some other evils that plague the system at your level or have a wider reach. One has to be careful here to separate the symptoms from the disease in identifying the malaise to target.

4. What you have left in your list is Category B - everything else!

So now all the points that you have listed out are in three categories - A, B and C.

Aggressively go after A, with equal determination pursue C, and with matched aggression and determination, firmly ignore B. Issues from Category B will keep cropping up every day of the year. The golden principle that applies here is 'The urgent crowds out the important' meaning that you end up fire-fighting only and never get to real policy issues in governance and contribute to development. In the field of photography for instance as Sri Chandra Babu Naidu and I noted in a discussion once (he was then the CM of Andhra Pradesh and I was the Chief Secretary), the meaning of 'focusing' upon an object before clicking the photograph Is that the rest of the picture should get blurred. Unless that blurring is achieved, one can never get the clarity over the focussed object. This is exactly like Arjuna seeing only the sparrow's eye in the mythical incident with Acharya Drona, while all other students who were asked to look at the tree saw so many things that they lost focus; seeing the tree, the colourful leaves, branches, even the feathers of the bird itself means that they did not achieve the desired blurring of everything else that was not the priority or focus. To ignore Category B, would be like enacting an Arjuna in your post!

You need to be able to avoid the "Grasshopper Mentality" -with your attention fitting from one thing to another and everything getting blurred.

Another danger to be wary of is the temptation to succumb to "time robbery". Those around you will often –and with perfectly good intentions, divert you away from the heart of the matter with a great deal of largely unnecessary details. This is just like placing, all of a sudden, an explanatory note in the hands of a speaker who is otherwise fully prepared with what he wants to say. It may be an attempt to assist him but usually disturb his concentration and probably impair the quality of the effort.

Once you know you have what you need you must resolutely spurn all input not germane to the achievement of your objective.

In order to keep abreast of things "monitoring of monitoring" can be done for this category - with the primary monitoring being done by the system and periodical checking taken up at your level. For this purpose, an occasional peep into the happenings of category B is also desirable.

As Chief Secretary the author started what was called the INSTAX (Instant Access to Exceptional Information) Station. Instead of relying on the slow and hierarchical flow of information, this station directly accessed information from the print and electronic media, the internet and also received telephonic messages, and mails, SMSs from field officers at the cutting-edge level of crucial departments. It had a well publicized mobile phone number and an E-mail ID. Field officers of important departments (Police, Drinking Water Supply, Medical and Health Services, Irrigation, Power and Roads etc.) had been given instructions to report details of any untoward or unusual occurrence (fire accidents, road accidents, building-collapses, flash floods etc.) directly to the station while separately sending formal reports in the prescribed form and through the proper channels.

The Station proved to an excellent asset. The December 26, 2004 Tsunami was preceded by a gradual rise in sea levels which was noticed in the villages on the coast of Andhra Pradesh State and reported through media. This information was first reported by the station, giving the system valuable time to ward off more damage than what actually took place.

In other words leave B for the system under you to grapple with.

Now looking at Categories A and C, you may find that there are far too many for your time even now. Categorize them further into Vital - do them first, Essential - hopefully get here, and Desirable - if you have the time. Open two tracks in your administration: One would be the day to day urgent Track 1, and the other would be the parallel, slow, but very firmly placed important Track 2. Create a small mechanism within your office to do nothing but the important track, in your name, with your authority but not directly by you, since you will be busy fire-fighting. This cell or mechanism must be monitored closely by you and should be given a clear destination, road-map and the milestones to achieve the end goals. Let them use your name and influence (Chief Secretary wants x, y, z, or Collector wants a, b, c to be done, etc) to get them to do their work which may include for example like an irrigation project, a thermal power station, a national high way, a large convention hall, a high tech city, a metro drinking water project, etc. Their list will consist of important long term development goals that will get constant and aggressive attention from the team. The system will respond to them since they have been created by you and their mechanism carries the influence of your office. But you need to visit them only at periodic intervals… a week, ten days, to check their progress and hurdles and the need for your intervention at various stages of your drafted milestones, roadmap and destination. It is important to cultivate the ability to remain engaged with the environment with a meaningful dialogue. It is only thus that you can stay in a proactive mode and not merely react to situations in a passive manner.

Slow but steady progress will hence be made for your Track 2 agenda while you are also able to deal with Track 1 that is inevitable. This means that you have effectively started putting in place a mechanism that will help you realise items from your

Category A and C, starting with the 'Vital' and moving into 'Essential' and 'Desirable' sub-categories through two clearly defined tracks of governance.

Bringing in an IAS officer as an Executive Assistant while the author was the Chief Secretary to the Government of Andhra Pradesh was one such endeavour. With their relatively higher status they were able to communicate freely with Secretaries, Heads of Departments and District Officers. And with the knowledge and experience already gained in the field they were able to add substantial speed and value to the processing of a handful of high priority items entrusted to them, while the Chief Secretary remained engrossed in day to day work. In others words the Executive Assistant spent his time seeing visions of international convention halls, mega multi-purpose hydro-electric projects and inter basin water transfers, underground railways and state - of - the art new airports and such like (many of which have translated into reality subsequently) – while yours truly was busy with tricky legislature questions vexatious, litigation, trade union demands census, elections etc., not to mention cyclones, fire accidents and extremism!

Your mantra is hence a simple ABC, VED and Twin-Track! You have simplified governance such that you can make meaningful contributions in any posting, and given any time frame, to the best of your abilities. But you have to take the 1st step to realising such a plan. You have to categorise and before that, you have to understand, do your homework, research and ask questions.

The author has, applied the system with spectacular results in many situations and departments. In the Commercial Tax Department a large number of petty cases, accounting for a majority of the number but making only an insignificant contribution to the revenue, were placed in category C. Similarly a very small number of cases involving huge amounts of revenue went into category A. Going after A and C improved, at once, the revenue collection as well as the overall disposal of cases, while the department attended to the remaining cases in category B. Likewise we analyzed the Urban Land Ceiling surplus area declarations in Hyderabad city in 1976. The ABC approach threw up more than 70% of trivial cases of excess land - small holders more or less accidentally crossing the bench- mark prescribed by the law - accounting as a group for a small extent of excess land (less than 5%) and going into category C. On the other hand less than 10% of the declarants together owned more than 50% of the total excess land and went into category A. The approach proved to be invaluable in providing immediate relief to a huge number of small holders sparing them from needless harassment and, simultaneously, allowed us to concentrate on the handful of worthwhile cases requiring careful and close scrutiny. Once again the remaining work (category B) was left to the system.

While all this analysis is essential there can, like all good things, be too much of it. Start with a tentative agenda on these lines and push ahead. Revisit this exercise once in a way and tweak it with benefit of knowledge gained as you go along. There is, otherwise, the danger of Xeno's paradox which deals with the following conundurum that half the distance between any two points has to be traversed in any journey, half of that distance again before proceeding further and so on until you conclude that no movement is possible! Similarly in administration, continuous or endless refinement of objectives could well end up preventing the exercise from beginning. Unless one begins to churn the milk the cream will not surface.

4. ETHICS AND GOVERNANCE IN AN EVER CHANGING WORLD

It is not the strongest of the species that survives, nor the most intelligent that survives, it is the one that is most adaptable to change

- Charles Darwin

4.1 Introduction

Change is inevitable. And so is the understanding and acceptance of ethics over time, with the constant testing and retesting of the validity of conventional wisdom as societies are subjected to change in the course of human history.

Change could be social, political or even technological, in the course of which, important truths though often deemed as outrageous when initially introduced, eventually integrate into the accepted wisdom of the times. Similarly, many respected values, considered mores, typically last a few decades before undergoing a process of adjustment caused by many factors including scientific findings, technological innovations, evolution of religious beliefs, changes in moral values, the persistence of vision-driven advocates, the perceptions of the media, changes in the economy, and demographic shifts.

Several sweeping transformations across societies have marked the process of the evolution of Ethics into the form and content it has assumed today.

Take for instance, the abolition of slavery, child-marriage, and dowry, or the introduction of birth-control methods, universal franchise and the attitude towards homosexuality, of legislatures and the judiciary, around the world. These are only some among the many illustrations of how Society has absorbed into its ethical mould, the altered perceptions of a civilisation from one era to the next. This has often been by way of a graceful embrace of the transition, sometimes by reconciliation with the inevitable and, on occasion, being overwhelmed and humbled by historical forces and violent compulsions forced upon the ethical framework, its prejudices swept away by a flood of resentment, by bitter struggle or, even bloodshed.

As the famous American poetess Maya Angelou said, "The needs of Society determine its ethics". Ethics change over time, and they do indeed evolve to reflect the changing needs of Society. Ethical behaviour ensures the well-being of Society and provides a bench-mark to discourage unhealthy and deviant behaviour in a dynamic milieu. It is therefore quite logical that ethical values should not remain rigid and inflexible; trapped, as it were, in a time-warp. They should remain open to the external environment, the times and the situations.

If the dictates of the evolutionary process are ignored beyond a point, a revolution will follow. In the process, however, a hardcore nucleus of values, such as truth and duty which stand the test of time will remain unaltered, recognised and acknowledged universally.

4.2 Traditional and Modern Ethics

It is important to realize that traditional and modern ethics are two faces of the same coin. One need to see them as they appear not as two contrasting values, but values linked and intertwined. Modern ethics could be perceived as a logical, natural development spurred on by traditional ethics. As times change, so do our ethical ideas and notions. What was wrong yesterday can be right now, and vice versa. This happens because our thinking evolves and transforms and it does not imply that ethics has lost its meaning. It is important to be abreast of the imperatives of changing times when dealing with ethical dilemmas.

4.3 Wars

Take wars for example. From the Vedic times, the ethical issues surrounding wars existed as did war itself, be it in the The Ramayana, The Mahabharata, or other mythological accounts not only in India but the world over. Ancient, medieval as well as modern times have been plagued by the scourge of war, be it Sudan, or Iraq post the terrorist attacks of 9/11 in New York City. Clearly, retaliation or deterrent punishment was a prime reason for war, as the Iraq War after the 9/11 incident. Similarly, even if Hiroshima-Nagasaki bombings are perceived by some as an ethically justifiable way in which nations behave, there perhaps need to be some norms about the quantum of retaliatory action, or restraint that nations may show. There is no 'plus or minus' answer to those ethical questions. Everything depends upon the side the perception originates from.

Even though war is sometimes inevitable, it is perhaps some consolation that people have at least agreed upon codes and conventions about how innocent people should be treated; soldiers for instance have nothing to do with political intentions, hence when they become POWs (Prisoners of War), standards such as the Geneva Convention may be called upon in dealing with them. In other words, ethics evolved out of war situations and its aftermath as well.

In this age of unparalleled change brought about by rapidly advancing technologies, people have to live with the consequences thereof. It is important to make good choices to minimize the adverse social, environmental and economic impacts of irresponsible use of technology. Informed ethical decision making and proactive assessment of effect of emerging technologies is essential.

While technologies in themselves are not capable of possessing moral or ethical qualities, industry and innovators need to consider the ethical issues involved.

The ethics of various human endeavours are influenced and changed by new technologies. The advent of bio engineering has brought in like preserving, cloning and implantation technologies. Many ethical questions have been raised in the wake of spread of these disciplines.

The emergence of ICT has similarly impacted on the right to privacy and the freedom of speech.

4.4 The Environment and Climate Change

Carbon sequestration for example is another good example of varied ethical values. How can a developed country force developing countries to accept their ethical values about carbon conservation where the utilization of coal leads to power, literacy, health care, welfare for women and children, etc. for instance as in India. For most developing countries, generating power in the short term unfortunately means you have to use carbon, or fossil fuels, since hydel energy is insufficient, nuclear energy has its limitations while other options are still being researched. Can a developing nation save the future at the cost of the present generation, especially in the context of widespread poverty, exploitation, and all that stems from it? Developed countries do not have as many pressing humanitarian implications, and can hence afford not to use carbon, just like the ethical values involved with WTO patents or intellectual property rights, pollution or even nuclear non-proliferation. Is it not easier for a country that has a nuclear weapon to stop producing more or to decrease its current stock, while it is quite not the same for a country exposed to risk of security.

Another example of the ethical debate follows the liberalisation, globalisation and privatisation of economies: the patent laws that do not restrict access to knowledge but discourage its use. They levy a premium on the use of knowledge that affects developing countries. The Vedas were the original examples of patenting: the exclusive preserve of a minority that people in general could not even access; they were passed on by word-of-mouth, only to a chosen few, and were esoteric to the commoner. Today however, they are all in the public realm and 'available' for everyone to read and assimilate.

Still access to that knowledge may require a certain amount of training or education. But then so does understanding biotechnology or the game of cricket!

4.5 Ethics in Emergency Management

Emergency Management (EM) is concerned with mitigation focused activities that form part of the EM continuum namely, - prevention, preparedness, rescue, relief and rehabilitation. The 2004 tsunami was a watershed eventin this regard. Poorly coordinated interaction between and amongst the governmental agencies, non-government organization (NGOs)/community based organization (CBOs) and other stake holders such as the corporate sector, the National Disaster Response Force (NDRF) etc. created a great deal of avoidable confusion ultimately resulting in causing greater distress to the victims.

Quite apart from promptness and efficiency, organizations charged with conducting EM operations need to ensure that their actions are informed by considerations of equity, fairness and positive discrimination in favour of special categorizes of victims such as women, children and the aged. They also have to modulate and harmonize the assistance offered by outside agencies which, though well intentioned, can sometimes have narrow or sectarian implications.

Ethics has a primary role to play in such a situation. And in the temporary absence of it, the self interest of the NGOs can take precedence and cause counter-productive results.

As a result of thought given to this imperative by researchers and NGOs, some guidelines have emerged including the following (Etkin& Davis, 2007):

- Humanitarian imperatives come first - This is especially important in serving the impoverished and the most deserving of the aid recipients.
- Aid output to be extended regardless of race, creed or nationality of the recipients and without discrimination of any kind.

Examples of duties that Etkin & Davis consider to be important are based on W.D Ross's "seven prima facie duties - namely,

- Beneficence – the duty to do good and promote happiness
- Malfeasance – the duty to do no harm and to prevent harm
- Fidelity – duties arising from past commitments and promises
- Reparation – duties that stem from past harms
- Gratitude – duties based upon past favors and unearned services
- Self improvement – the duty to improve our knowledge and virtue
- Justice – the duty to give each person equal consideration
- Retributive justice – punishment for wrongdoing
- Distributive justice – fair distribution of benefits and burdens

These ethical dimensions are expected to help resolve dilemmas that those discharging functions face in an emergency..Their application, as can be seen, can lead to achieving the much needed balance between quality and efficiency on the one hand and serving the needs of the most deserving on the other.At the same time, they also help balance the priorities between the short and the long terms. At the same time ethical considerations in EMalso help set standards for future relief and aid. This is essential because this would take into consideration not just the economic impact of disasters and the wealth lost by those but also consider the pain and suffering.

4.6 Whistle Blowers

The role of whistle blowers is worth mentioning in this context. Arvind Kejriwal started as one in India. So did Ralph Nader six decades ago in the USA leading crusade against misleading advertisements, defects in products, etc., of many reputed multinationals of that time. Such persons become self-appointed umpires raising questions in the public interest with no personal motive or benefit and have an important role in the emergence of ethics and changes in existing standards. Of course, every one cannot be a whistle blower, unless one has the reputation, attitude or influence to make one heard. Often times, the whistle may not be heard, and one may decide to just go on with one's own life without championing a cause.

Judicial pronouncements, especially in India have had their impact on the evolution of ethical standards; as witness, the recent pronouncements of the Supreme Court of India on issues such as the status of transgender individuals or the legitimacy of the offspring of "live in" couples.

Ethics is a complex and highly subjective discipline, very much influenced by the point of view of the person who is practicing it. It is unlike a science such as chemistry or physics which remains unaltered for everyone. So it helps not to be overenthusiastic about putting in place a rigid and inflexible code of ethics that would clearly tell everyone what is right and wrong. Henry Adams, the famous American historian once said that morality 'is a private and costly luxury'; in a lighter vein, don't take your morality outside your house and get beaten up, and practise it only if you can afford to!

4.7 Corporate Governance

Management is about the choice, evaluation and implementation of optimal strategies, sound policies and appropriate procedures most suited to achieving pre-determined goals. It is an art concerned with doing things in the best manner possible and involves supervision of performance, and getting into the granular details concerning the quantity and quality of output. Ethics help lay down the principles that govern ethical responsibilities of public servants. This in turn reinforces the existing facets of ethics at the workplace and contributes to both the normative and descriptive elements of ethics. These aspects are crucial for strengthening confidence among the general public in the public servant's commitment to ethical conduct.

Research has pointed to two distinct approaches to managing ethics at the workplace - namely, compliance - centric and integrity - centric. The "compliance" approach to ethics management is based on external controls on public servants and relies largely on formal and detailed rules and procedures. These external controls also comprise legislations, codes and other procedures. The "integrity" approach focuses on internal controlsor the individual's capacity for making moral judgment. The integrity approach also lays emphasis on situations which are confronted on a daily basis. Internal controls also rely on moral development and judgments. Moral development comprises values, beliefs, perceptions etc. while judgment is subjective and is dependent on adherence to certain universal laws.

These points are crucial because they also aid governance in the proper management of the organizations and enterprises; for instance, in functions such as recruitment and training. Arthur Andersen was once one of the former "big 5" accounting firms internationally. An ethical crisis was precipitated when the principals of the firm were alleged to have fudged their books of account in order to overstate profits.

It is in this context that the long term impact of questionable organizational practices came to light. The company's slide into ignominy actually started some nine years before the event that sealed its fate - when a series of accounting scandals broke out and cases came to light pertaining to obstruction of justice, - exposing an underlying corporate culture that nurtured unethical practices. This was in stark contrast to the unsullied image associated with the firm since its inception. Organizational values succumbed to the temptation of making profit at any cost and principles were relegated to the background. The decay was hastened by the influx of a new breed of auditors and accountants whose value - system had been compromised by the pressure to undertake window – dressing exercises to inflate profits.

"Power corrupts and absolute power corrupts absolutely", said Lord Action. Such, at that time, was Arthur Andersen's influence in high places, that it was able to adversely impact on the working of the Professional Standards Group which oversaw the accounting and auditing practices in USA.

Arthur Andersen was further involved in the downfall of the Houston, Texas - based oil giant - Enron. Enron's unethical practices included the exploitation of accounting loopholes, improper financial reporting, and manipulation to sweep under the carpet billions of dollars of debt caused by failed deals and projects. In addition some key executives such as the Chief Financial Officer misled Enron's board of directors and its audit committee on the wisdom of adopting high-risk accounting practices. Acclaimed researchers like Healey & Palepu in their paper assessing the governance practices of Enron have averred that the company was able to fund a questionable business model, conceal its true performance through artificial accounting, and boost stock values artificially leading to the inevitable downfall.

Codes of ethics are fairly well developed in Sweden in comparison to other parts of the world. Many multi-national companies based in Sweden not only have ethical codes in place but also undertaken several complementary initiatives in place to ensure that organizational cultures are ethically sound.

From a governance perspective, ethics help guide enterprises in their dealings in the marketplace, serve as a guiding point for strategic planning and therefore secure a range of benefits. This is seen as crucial in light of some researchers' findings that unethical decision making was more prevalent when negative perceptions pervaded the ambience of organizations they were part of - the counter point to the view that positive perceptions foster the making of ethical choices.

Moral climate is also determined by the actions of the leadership. Ethics researchers Sims & Brinkmann point out how the former CEO of Enron, Jeff Skilling helped create a climate in which failure would not be tolerated - a factor that contributed significantly to a high degree of unethical decision making across different levels of the organization. They further point to the following factors which contributed adversely to the dilution of ethics:

- Extreme focus on the short term and on the making of profit at any cost
- Blame culture in the organization that clouded ethical decision making at all levels within the organization
- Initiation of illegal practices by the top management
- themselves ignoring employees concerns and
- the same time a willingness to overlook improper behaviour for securing questionable gains.

Public servants chosen to be custodians of organizational ethics would need to possess a degree of specialized competence and credentials appropriate for performing that function. Persons with a thorough understanding of the working of the organization would naturally be able to guide employees better on such matters. This could be considered a core qualification. Perhaps an even more important requirement would be the ability to face crises firmly and a commitment to integrity. Interpersonal skills in handling conflicts and a knack for building relationships with all stakeholders including whistleblowers would be an added advantage.

PSUs in India

Public Sector Undertakings (PSUs) in India have for long had a major role to play in the process of growth and development. 97 "Maharatna" companies and "Mini ratnas" come under the ambit of the Department of Public Enterprises, Government of India. The general perception is that the performance of the PSUs leaves much to be desired in many spheres including the realization of their missions, promptness, efficiency, and a commitment to probity on the part of the employees.

Given the high level of expectations from these undertakings (albeit with mandates restricted in the wake of the emergence of the forces of liberalization, privatization and globalization following structural economic reforms post 1991) the long neglected exercise of ensuring enhanced levels of performance and increased accountability from these organizations needs to be addressed as an important and urgent national priority.

4.8 Ethics & compliance

Building a strong ethical culture plays a significant role in preparing individual employees to successfully deal with ethical challenges. A committed leadership, comprising individuals fit to be role models worthy of emulation, is a sine qua non for undertaking such a task. Those at the top need to put in place standards and bench marks for to be integrated into the process of governance. The top management has also the responsibility of infusing ethical practices into the mission and vision statements of the organization so that the right signals are sent into the ethos of the system.

Care should, of course be taken to ensure that the role of officials charged with ensuring compliance to a code of ethics is a substantial one and not merely symbolic. Integrating ethics into the work culture of an institution requires many initiatives including:

- Putting in place appropriate checks and balances
- Instituting mechanism for reporting incidents that constitute violation of ethics
- Meting out exemplary punishment for malfeasance and misconduct

Conflict of Interest

A conflict of interest is defined as an action or relationship that can make an employee's action subjective and interfere with the ability to make fair decision. An employee of a computer sales company who starts a side business with identical operations will clearly cause diversion of valuable business away from the company. At the same time, the employee's abilities, resources and time are being utilized for promoting an activity that competes with that of the organization employing him. This evidently is a case conflict of interest.

Conflict of interest can arise on the part of the public servant when discrimination, arbitrariness and mala fides colour the exercise of authority. Unless dealt with promptly and severely such conflict can severely undermine the interests of the organization.

Ethical Governance

In the new millennium, the challenges facing the world are forever growing in number and complexity. These encompass a whole gamut of issues--technical, financial, security-related, environmental and others- that are faced by civil servants and common people alike. With globalization and privatization society is presented with a bewildering variety of choices and hopeful outcomes, demanding principled leadership and institutional creativity in delivering public services. Governance has continuously to deal with expectations of citizens, while also evaluating the criteria of efficiency, effectiveness, economy and value.

Ethics in Governance is often not a simple choice between right and wrong. Public servants need to be particularly concerned about the ethical quality of decisions taken while discharging their duties because society at large can be affected by their outcome, impacting not merely individuals but millions of people, perhaps forever. Ethical governance is about how one applies theoretical values to practical decisions which can affect a large number of people for a long time.

4.9 Rethinking Governance in an ever Changing World

"For forms of government let fools contest, whatever is best administered, is best", said Alexander Pope.

Expectations from governments and their institutions run high all over the world. Good governance helps create an environment that enables economic growth and hastens social development in a manner consistent with the needs of sustainability. It is thus associated with enlightened political leadership, a supportive policy framework and a committed administration marked by professional excellence.

In his famous 'tryst with destiny' speech on 14 August 1947, Jawaharlal Nehru articulated the challenge facing the country as 'the ending of poverty and ignorance and disease and inequality of opportunities'.

It is the view of this author that after the onset of the era of structural reforms, post 1990, India has transited from the "growth with justice" paradigm that characterized the economic doctrine of the initial Mahalanobis model to a mode of governance informed by the "growth and justice" pattern.

India is striving to achieve a high growth rate with a focus on equity. These objectives are not always contradictory. Conflict, however, arises when scarce resources are diverted to meet the demands of the growing middle class or the affluent sections, to the exclusion of the poor. Until now a good deal of emphasis in governance has been on the resolution of individual issues or refinement of processes within government institutions. This is beginning to change. People are engaging more and more actively with public issues and are not afraid to stand up for what is right and ethical, increasing the demand for ethical governance.

Enhancing the quality of governance is a vital issue that affects every citizen. No theory of governance would be relevant unless it is seen in the context of its time. In the new millennium, it has become evident that those who want minimal government are gaining an upper hand over the advocates of the paternalist welfare state. But there is no visible shortcut to runaway success in sight. It is being increasingly accepted that a democratic form of government is the best bet to ensure justice and equity together with the pursuit of the goals of growth and development. Similarly, there is also emphasis on the fact that the administrative systems have to be regionally differentiated and respond to the varying demands in a country marked by diversity and complexity caused by several factors. Non-state actors have also rightly begun to occupy more and more role space in the realm of governance. Thus a system that is robust, flexible and embraces a plural and decentralized regime is the need of the hour. The principal role of the state would be to facilitate, enable, and coordinate. It must be realized that neither the market nor the civil society can become substitutes for the government in the handling of core governmental functions of a purely regulatory nature.

The task here is not to take sides with various ethical debates but to raise issues- flag them, not deal with them or suggest solutions. A word of caution against the dimension and complexity involved in the practice of ethics and in the preaching of it: What does not change as moral values change has lost its use perhaps. The recent Supreme Court rulings on homosexuality or the children of live-in parents in India would have been taboo till just a few years ago.

It is no doubt necessary to understand what Jesus Christ preached, or what Lord Krishna said to Arjuna, what Mohammad advised his followers to do, or even what Confucius or Gandhiji asked of people. What is much more important is what they would have said had they been alive today. We must contemporise their views, project their philosophies into the real world of today, onto our plane of existence, and see what these projections look like before we imbibe them or deal with them.

Since crime is a function of the laws in vogue, we should remember Thoreau's exhortation "*...simplify, simplify, simplify...*"

Old order must change yielding place to new in the words of celebrated English poet Lord Alfred Tennyson. And as Hegel famously theorized, thesis and anti-thesis must interact, culminating in a synthesis, either by evolution or by revolution.
The choice is ours.

One last word...

Ethics in Governance – from dreams to reality

Ethics is an integral part of governance, the definition of Ethics varying over time and space. In the Indian subcontinent, Ethics has been deeply rooted in the approach of the rulers since times immemorial as evidenced by the Vedic scriptures which preached "Vasudaiva Kutumbam" - universal brotherhood and the establishment of - peace and harmony among the subjects.

The Puranas such as the Ramayana, followed by the Mahabharata, had evolved from the Vedas. The exemplary rule of King Rama was universally acknowledged as an ideal form of governance (Rama Rajyam). While the Ramayana highlighted Dharmic values in governance, the Mahabharata emphasized the principles of good administration such as Raja Neeti and the need for the conduct of the King towards the people to be informed by ethical values.

Chanakya is perhaps the only person acknowledged as a genius by Indian, Oriental as well as Western scholars. His work represents a historical milestone in the making of India traversing which we observe many upheavals and myriad reversals. His book "Arthashastra" clearly defines the functions of all the people involved in public administration and remains relevant even today.

Medieval India saw the regimes of many great rulers like Akbar, Prithvi Raj Chouhan, Sher Shah Suri, among others. This period saw the ushering in of many reforms and farsighted measures intended for the welfare of people and development of the kingdom. Ministers like Raja Todar Mal during Akbar's times introduced the concept of standard weights and measures. Many of the methods of data collection practiced over the centuries in the Indian subcontinent and neighboring countries are informed by the features of his initiatives. The provision of ethical governance was the underlying objective all through.

After Independence, Government of India, following the recommendations of various Committees, initiated several measures to improve the efficiency of administration. Nearly all of them rely on the conviction that ethical and moral actions should remain the guiding principle of Good Governance. The mandate of the first Administrative Reforms Commission headed by Shri Morarji Desai initially and later on by Shri K.Hanumanthaiah, included a study of Ethics in Governance and proposed the setting up of a Lokpal. The second Commission, which was headed by Shri Verrappa Moily, also submitted a report on Ethics in Governance. The practice of professions such as Medicine, Accountancy and the Law is regulated by self-imposed standards and codes.

As the world entered a new millennium, society is confronted with imposing challenges, fateful choices and hopeful outcomes, demanding principled leadership and institutional creativity in delivering public services. Today there are so many conflicting demands being made on professional public servants that they have to prioritize and choose among several competing value sets. Which particular set is preferred depends on cultural socialization, political regime, social conditions, economic pressures, institutional arrangements, peer group pressure, organization culture/bureaucratization, and even personal conscience. Again which set is employed varies from country to country, regime to regime, government to government, organization to organization, according to the conditions at any particular point of time and the nature of the organization's activities, supporting groups, vested interests and clientele, not just internal rules, group norms and individual preferences.

The Governance has to continuously measure up to the expectations of citizens, combined with the evaluation criteria of efficiency, effectiveness, economy and value. In fact, the economic conception of public service leads us to the idea of delivering a good or a service below its cost, not forgetting quality and the essential factors named above. The outcomes are obviously imperative, but Public Administration "must, primarily, have the duty to observe the legality of its acts and to respect the citizens' rights and needs" with ethically responsible conduct as a fundamental factor of evaluation.

The time has come to move from dreams to reality. Personal ethics cannot be separated from the public context in which most of us are destined to spend the majority of our lives, be it working for the private sector or a government department. The lessons of ethics are learned throughout our lives as we associate with others and play a very important role in influencing the personal and professional conduct of people and the functioning of the Society as a whole.

The very survival of Society as an independent, democratic, prosperous and sustainable organism depends on the ability of its members and its public servants to maintain the high ethical standards.

The challenge, however, lies in ensuring that ethical values are followed and applied in our daily lives, and in particular, in matters relating to governance. 'Ethics in Governance' essentially refers to customary values and rules of conduct in public administration - including selflessness, integrity, objectivity, accountability, openness, honesty and leadership.

If ethics were easy and straightforward in governance and delivery of public services, there would be no need for books such as this one. However, this is rarely the case. Ethical decision making and practice are fraught with difficulties and challenges in governance. Ethics often stretches and moves the public servants to think beyond their own self to consider others in society. Public servants need to ask themselves on their own ethical position or stance. They need to think on about actions and both intended and unintended consequences. These are challenging questions appears to be personal level but can become complex, if not daunting.

One of the goals of this book is to raise awareness regarding many of the common-sense assumptions about public servants particularly when it comes to ethics. After reading this book, I hope it improves the awareness to pursue ethical questions and help to establish one's own views on ethics in governance.

It is not just enough to be aware of ethics in public service delivery but it also requires strong critical thinking skills to understand ethical situations and possible courses of action. The case studies are expected to help learning about ethical theories, in general, and ethical practices, specifically. Further, they help to have greater confidence in decision making and to better understand the decisions of others. Finally, a third goal is to motivate you to respond to, and proactively confront, ethical dilemmas that may arise in delivery of public services. Overall, it is hoped that, after reading this book, one believes that ethics in governance matters and it is essential to use knowledge, skill, and motivation to enhance the ethics in governance.

All through this book I have tried to provide a holistic view of ethics and its importance to governance especially in relation to the dilemmas faced by public servants while performing their duties in a challenging environment.

Optimism has forever been my weakness. I feel confident that this small effort will serve as a useful instrument in the hands of those responsible for providing a proactive, responsive, accountable and efficient administration in a participatory and inclusive mode.

In the preface to this book I expressed the hope that it will, in the future, become a part of a process of change for the better. Such change, one trusts, will last and endure. I say this because – *"plus ça change, plus c'est la même chose"* "the more it changes, the more it remains the same"- goes the somewhat cynical saying in French. It is to be hoped that this will prove wrong in regard to the transformation we all look forward to.

Mohan Kanda

5. CASE STUDIES

Covered in this section are two categories of illustrations.

In the first part are incidents drawn from the experience of the author which are presented in a narrative form. Each incident covers an aspect of governance related to day to day life.

Placed in the second part are some illustrative questions circulated by the Union Public Service Commission of India for the benefit of those preparing for the Civil Services Examinations as also the actual problems as they appeared in the Civil Services Mains General Studies Paper 4: Ethics, Integrity & Aptitude. Clearly the approaches recommended for responding to these problems are hypothetical and cannot, in the nature of things, be considered either unique or universally applicable.

5.1 Real Time Situations

1. Result versus Procedure

"Karman Eva Adhikaraste Maa Phaleshu Kadaachanaa"

Says Lord Krishna to Arjuna in the Bhagvatgita - emphasizing the importance of doing one's duty and not worrying about the result.

Civil Servants, similarly, must follow the rules and procedures in force while performing their functions in any situation, no matter how challenging.

This incident dates back to 1972. General elections were being held and I was Sub Collector at Ongole in Prakasham District, Andhra Pradesh. I was also the Returning Officer for Parchur Assembly Segment.

It was a tensely fought election marked by violent incidents. X of the ruling Congress-I party and another candidate Y were locked in a close contest. On the day of the counting, X was in hospital in Guntur town following injuries sustained in a clash. When the counting concluded, X trailed by 250 out of a total of about 50,000 thousand votes. He promptly requested a recount as provided in the Electoral Law.

My immediate impulse would normally have been to automatically agree the request. But the situation called for a dispassionate review of the procedure and arrangements that we followed during the counting: (Number of tables: 2 more than the required; number of counting assistants and supervisors - more than prescribed; agents of both parties present at every table and at the counting hall, RO (myself) and the Assistant Returning Officers did a good deal more than the prescribed percentage of checking, all disputed ballot papers duly settled as per procedure!

The ethical question to answer was not whether the result itself was accurate, but whether the result emerged from the procedure laid down and the prescribed precautions. The duty of the RO is to organize counting, not to count the votes! Feeling that what was required had been done the request for a recount was rejected referring to the procedures and precautions as listed above through a speaking order.

Mr. X challenged the result in the High Court, and subsequently a recount was ordered by the Court. Mr. X however polled less!

2. The Power of Persuasion and Parley

In 1972, at the peak of the Andhra Agitation, once again during my tenure as Sub-Collector Ongole, 1972, Dr. K.L. Rao, the then Union Minister of State for Water Resources in the Congress I Government was passing through Chirala (which was in my jurisdiction) enroute to Delhi from Chennai. As was the custom, I had to receive him at the railway station and extend to him official courtesies. The halt was uneventful, and I returned to the Guest House at Chirala soon after. I was informed that the train was held up at the outer signal, by a handful of students. Their demand was for Dr. K.L. Rao to say 'Jai Andhra!'

I rushed to the spot, entered the train compartment and spoke to Dr. Rao. I convinced him to express his empathy with the act of the students without making a commitment on the demand per se (as that was clearly not possible), and assure them that their demand for a separate state would be conveyed to the Central Government. Mentally prepared to stay calm while meeting the students, I walked up to them, recognised and hailed a prominent leader amongst them. After putting them at ease, I explained that the incident as had transpired until then was adequate for calling public attention to their cause, and I pointed out to them the futility of prolonging the act of holding up the train - causing inconvenience and anger to hundreds of passengers. In effect I struck a deal with them to desist from pressing for the Minister to join them with a slogan but to settle for an assurance that he would convey their sentiments to the Government of India.

The issue thus settled, the train was allowed to proceed and we bid farewell to the Minister!

3. **Bureaucrats should also think out of the box sometimes!- Work 'on' the system instead of merely 'in it'**

In 1975, I was posted as The Deputy Commissioner (Commercial Taxes) of the Kurnool Division (comprising Kurnool and Anantapur Districts) of Andhra Pradesh state.

Sales Tax is tax levied on transaction relating to the sale or purchase of goods or services. Entrainment Tax is levied on a per person basis on the organizers (exhibitors) of movies, plays, circuses, amusement parks etc. There was no provision originally enabling the department to make an "assessment" in cases of suspicion of evasion of entertainment tax, all though such a provision was available in respect to sales tax. A provision empowering the department to make such assessment was brought in in 1974. There was still no provision for making the "best judgment" and, therefore, to raise a demand in respect or suppressed transactions and asses/collect the revenue thereupon. Thus, tax once lost on the passage of the event could neither be levied nor collected subsequently.

Typically the revenue from ET is ploughed back from the State's exchequer to the coffers of local bodies such as Urban Local Bodies or Panchyati Raj Institutions.

In respect of movies the rights of distribution are usually acquired for a price from the producer by the distributors for different parts of the state of country and then sold again to individual exhibitors in cities, towns and villages.

Evasion of ET was known to be of a very high order. The exhibitors used to put forth many reasons - including power failure, projector or malfunction, stoppage of the show on account of rain (in temporary structures such as tents – common in those days), the failure of rail or bus transport to deliver the film reels etc., in order to suppress the attendance and therefore, the tax payable. Often, entry tickets with seal of the CT department were not sold and cash collected in lieu thereof, with a view to declaring a lower figure of gross income to the CT department.

In order to appreciate the magnitude and spread of evasion of ET, I under took to organize a series of continuous inspections of theaters in the division. The assistance of both the District Collectors was enlisted to request all touring officers across all Departments to incorporate a visit to a theater in their tours and fill up a small cheque memo created by the CT department.

The information collected, after being collated, suggested a high order of evasion and a huge gap between the known expenditure (power consumption, salaries, carbons use in the projector, maintenance of the premises, salaries etc.) and their declined incomes in effect most theaters reported a negative income and paid no tax.

All the distributors pertaining to Kurnool division had their offices at Guntakal town. I organized a simultaneous raid of all their 17 premises. When the collection particulars brought in from the raids were cross-verified with reported figures from the theatres, it was possible to compute the hypothetical loss of ET on the basis of assumption that no theater would run below break-even point. Notices were then issued to the exhibitors demanding payment of the tax "loss".

Clearly these notices were based on an assumption which, unlike in the case of ST, was without legal sanctity or legitimacy. Naturally the act was received with bitter resentment and anger and no compliance thereon followed.

In order to precipitate matters I carried the operation to its logical conclusion and on the expiry of the date prescribed for the payment of the tax, ordered the inspection and closure of theaters in Guntakal of peak show time following the discovery of a minor violation of the conditions of the exhibitor's license (as the non-payment of the tax demanded could not be a legitimate ground for such action).

In short my action was only marginally less than high handed all though inspired by conviction based on the principles of natural justice. All the exhibitors spontaneously declared an independent "strike" and all theaters in both districts were shut down abruptly. The impasse lasted for over fifty (50) days across more than one hundred and fifty (150) theaters.

Following a representation made by the exhibitors, the state government deputed Sri A. Krishna Swamy, IAS, First Member (as the office was then known) of the Board of Revenue (also the Commissioner, CT) to inquire into the matter. CCT gave exhibitors a patient hearing. He concluded by telling them that since the service offered by them was not like that extended by a hospital or a school, and also as their activity was not in the nature of running a public utility such as the supply of drinking water or power, it was an entirely up to them to decide whether or not to run their theaters and he returned to Hyderabad (state headquarters).

When nothing was heard of for some time and, compelled by commercial considerations, the exhibitors commenced running of the theaters.

As a matter of fact, the ET law was there after amended with retrospective effect introducing a new provision for "best judgment assessment!"

This was subsequently followed by another policy reform by way of introducing the "slab" system where levy of entertainment tax in theater was fixed not on the per capita or entry basis but on the basis of the classification of the theater in accordance with parameters including, among others, the population of the city, town or village.

What had originally started out as a curiosity driven study spurred on by suspicion went viral, assumed critical mass and ended in an amendment of the law impacting a fundamental aspect of the levy and collection of Entertainment Tax.

4. Standing one's ground – the value of building a consensus

This incident is from my early days as a Member of the National Disaster Management Authority (NDMA).

In 2005, soon after superannuation as Chief Secretary, Government of Andhra Pradesh I was appointed as a Member of the National Disaster Management Authority (NDMA), a new body constituted under the Disaster Management Act 2005. The Prime Minister is the Chairman of NDMA which has eight (8) other members, one of whom (at that time Gen N.C. Vij, formerly Chief of Army Staff) is appointed as the Vice Chairman. The Vice Chairman has the rank of a Union Cabinet Minister while the other Members have the rank and status of Union Ministers of State.

In the very first meeting held in Centaur Hotel in New Delhi (where NDMA was temporarily located to begin with), discussions began on the drafting of a National Policy on Disaster Management.

Apparently the then Home Minister wanted the newly constituted body to prepare the draft of such a Policy. The discussion centered round the manner in which a skeleton (three to four pages) draft earlier attempted by the Ministry of Home Affairs, Government of India, could be enriched, in form and content and passed on to the Central Government for approval. The timeframe being mentioned was three to four days!

New as I was to the environment and unfamiliar with the persuasions of the others, I was at a loss to appreciate the workability of the proposal. How could a National Policy be attempted in a matter of days, especially in a field that largely represented uncharted territory and pertained to a vital and grave concern?

Just when the discussion was about to conclude with only procedural aspects, remaining to be the settled, I took the courage of my conviction in hand and stated my views.

Any such policy, I pointed out, needed to be drafted in a participatory and inclusive manner capturing.

- the essence of all that so far transpired.
- outlining the residual issues remaining on the national agenda and
- describing precisely the contours of the destination the policy aims to reach, together with the road-map thereto complete with time-lines and milestones.

I insisted that such a task would have to involve closely the other ministries/departments of the Central Government, the State Governments scientific and technical organisations, academic institutions, the corporate sector and representatives of Civil Society Based Organizations and Non-Governmental Organizations. The Vice Chairman and other Members agree to think the matter over.

I spent the evening conferring with senior colleagues of mine, in particular Sri J. Harinarayan, then Union Secretary of Water Resources and Dr. V.K. Agnihotri, who subsequently served as Secretary General of the Rajya Sabha. The latter had, in fact, a Doctorate to his credit in the field of Public Policy from the Indian Institute of Technology, Delhi.

I fielded Dr. Agnihotri in the discussion that ensued the next day. He made a brilliant presentation on the ingredients of good public policy and the most acceptable method of putting it in place. Thereupon, the Authority agreed to pursue the line of action suggested by me and to inform the Home Minister that the exercise would take some more time.

I subsequently headed a "Core Group" constituted for the purpose and proceeded with the task. It took nearly three years!

Compensation, however, lay in the acknowledgement by one and all that the draft of the Policy that emerged from the deliberations of that group had an enduring quality and lasting value. The all-important ownership, on the part of all the stakeholders, was also ensured.

In fact the procedure followed by that group (which was also endorsed by the Authority) became a Standard Operating Procedure (SOP) for all documents which the NDMA was tasked to prepare in the future and, after some modifications became known as the "nine-step process".

Thus an important document dealing with a critical area of public policy came into being, though not in the manner originally conceived and not within the time-limit initially contemplated.

Standing one's ground and securing consensus for a radically-different course of action proved worth the while in the long-run.

5. The Holy Debate - Accountability Vs. Responsibility

I took over as Secretary (Agriculture and Cooperation) Government of India in January 2003. Both the promotion and the posting were events long awaited. It was my dream assignment! I was eagerly looking forward to putting to good use the close to three year tenure I would have in that post. In March 2003, Sri N. Chandrababu Naidu, then the Chief Minister of Andhra Pradesh mooted the idea of my returning to the State as Chief Secretary. Irrespective of my personal feelings my reaction was to leave the choice to him. By the end of that month I took over the new assignment.

The Chief Minister had already been in place for over six years and was fully familiar with the people, the places and the issues. I had to work hard to create some 'role-space' for myself in the affairs of governance. Just as I settled and carved out an ambitious agenda for myself, the run-up began for the conduct of the Pushkarams of the Godavari River - a prestigious and logistically challenging event that occurs once in twelve years and attracts crowds in the lakhs, mainly in Rajahmundry town on the banks of the river. It was a mammoth exercise requiring an enormous amount of coordination and team work involving nearly all the departments of the State Government. I jumped into the fray with enthusiasm and commenced making the requisite elaborate and careful arrangements for the pilgrims wanting to bathe in the holy waters of the Godavari. The Pushkarams went off very well and we were all satisfied with the arrangements.

A year later, in 2004 Dr. Y.S. Rajasekhar Reddy was the new Chief Minister of Andhra Pradesh, and I, as the Chief Secretary took the lead for putting in place the arrangements for the ensuing Pushkarams of the Krishna River. The main place of pilgrimage was Vijayawada town, on the banks of the River in Krishna District. Thanks to the experience with the Godavari Pushkarams the year before, the air was full of confidence and expectation of another good performance. Also was the added element of a new Government out to prove its capabilities.

In the early hours of the morning of the day on which the event was to commence, a report was received that four people drowned and lost their lives in an accident near the barrage across the Krishna River at Vijayawada. As a matter of fact the formal inauguration of the event had not yet taken place. The accident occurred at a spot which was not one of the venues designated for pilgrims to bathe and engage in their rituals. Apparently a group of people went to an unprotected place where water was being discharged and were washed away. In fact the event did not seem to have any connection with the Pushkarams as such.

I was upset and angry. While the administration was not at fault, the incident was precisely of the sort that was sought to be avoided throughout the preparatory period; I was devastated at this inauspicious prelude to the event.

The Chief Minister was on tour, at the temple town of Srisailam at that time. I called him, briefed him about the incident and also offered to proceed on leave as I felt that the government had to accept accountability for the event and I had taken a prominent and leading role in putting the arrangements in place. The Chief Minister promptly brushed aside my suggestion and asked me for suggestions about the immediate course of action.

The Chief Minister was about to leave Srisailam for Vijayawada by a helicopter to inaugurate the event formally. Upon arrival he would naturally have been accosted by the media. Vijayawada has always been a political nerve-centre of the State. The media, especially in a situation such as this, would not settle for a weak or routine reaction. In the wake of the allegations made by the media about the ineffective arrangements made by the State for the festival, we had to handle the issue of 'accountability' (not to be confused with the issue of 'responsibility'). I advised the Chief Minister that:

(a) the District Collector of Krishna District (in which Vijayawada town is located) be asked proceed on leave – as he was the head of the system tasked with the conduct of the event and also to pave the way for a fair investigation into the circumstances that led to the event.

(b) the Police Commissioner of Vijayawada be transferred out – to facilitate an impartial inquiry into the matter.

(c) the Superintending Engineer in charge of the Krishna Barrage be kept under suspension – as being prima facie accountable for the incident.

(d) an enquiry be ordered into the whole event by the Chief Commissioner Land Administration (the senior most officer after the Chief Secretary in the administrative hierarchy).

The District Collector of Krishna was a sound and hardworking officer whose qualities I held in great regard for. So was the Commissioner of Police of Vijayawada. The Superintending Engineer was an efficient officer who had put his heart and soul into the arrangements. And, the administration was in no way 'responsible' for what had happened. Still the question of 'accountability' remained and, in the face of the tragedy that occurred, the government had to be seen as accepting accountability and responding accordingly.

Upon arrival at Vijayawada the Chief Minister straightaway announced all the decisions taken. The nature and degree of the response of the government was such that no unpleasant repercussions followed and the Chief Minister's programme went through uneventfully.

The inquiry showed what was anticipated, that no human error or official lapse caused the incident. Subsequently the District Collector was reposted to his assignment and the Superintending Engineering honourably absolved of any failure on his part. At a time like that and at a politically volatile place such as Vijayawada, such an event would normally have caused extreme embarrassment to the government and marred the excellent arrangements. The response ensured that there was no undesirable fallout. It also teaches us that accepting accountability and being let off after inquiry is essential and desirable, rather than fighting the allegations and losing control over a situation.

6. More Loyal then the King! – Political will triumphs

I was posted as Commissioner of Excise, Government of Andhra Pradesh in the year 1987. Sri N.T. Rama Rao was the Chief Minister.

I was a rather reluctant occupant of that post on account of an inbuilt dislike for regulatory assignments (of which, needless to say, there has been no shortage in my career!). I consoled myself that it was essentially a linear and incremental function to levy and collect revenue, only doing it better than before. Performance and success would be easily amenable to recognition.

The department dealt with levy and collection of State Excise duty on toddy, arrack and Indian Made Foreign Liquor, apart from performing certain other miscellaneous functions entrusted to it. The revenue from the sale of arrack constituted not only a major chunk of the department's total revenue but was also a substantial part of the state's receipts.

Soon after I took over a radical change in the Excise Policy was being discussed at the highest levels. The idea was to do away with the system of auctioning the rights of sale of arrack by individual shops or groups and to switch over to a system whereby the sellers would be selected and appointed by the government, - and an ad valorem duty collected on the actual value of arrack sold (as against the extant system of the seller paying the amount promised in the auction).

Prima facie, the proposal looked dangerous to me. The revenue may be put at risk and the process of selection was fraught with potential for interference and could cause a flood of complaints.

At that time Sri Chandrababu Naidu (subsequently the Chief Minister of Andhra Pradesh), was the Chairman of the Rashtra Karshaka Parishad with the rank and status of a

Cabinet Minister. He was also the General Secretary of the ruling Telugu Desam Party and had an important role to play in policy matters in general. In particular he was interested in pushing the reform in question, which was seem as a measure of freeing the arrack trade from the grip of monopolies and allowing the revenue to realize its actual potential. At his instance we met in his office to discuss to proposed policy correction. While I appreciated the spirit behind the change I remained unconvinced about its workability and wary of the consequences. Sri Naidu indicated during the discussion that the change would come inevitably, and unless I changed my attitude, I would merely be seen as its sole opponent. I politely pointed out him that I valued my conviction much more than the satisfaction of being on the winning side of a debate.

A meeting of the state cabinet considered the proposal. When the subject came up for discussion the Principal Secretary Revenue (my immediate superior), the Principal Secretary Finance, the Chief Secretary and the Minister of Excise all had no specific views to offer; perhaps they had had an earlier discussion and were convinced of the need to approve the proposal. Just as the Chief Minister was about to treat the matter as approved and pass on to the next item, I put my hand up and requested a hearing. NTR was not happy as he had heard of my reservations and was not pleased with my wanting to air them at that forum. I stood my ground and NTR reluctantly acquiesced. I spoke my duly rehearsed piece, listing out all my objections pointing to the pit falls and highlighting my apprehensions; the minute I concluded, NTR passed on to the next item. I called on the Chief Secretary soon thereafter and requested to be relieved of the post in view of my stand on the matter. The Chief Secretary counselled me with the fairly standard advice given in such circumstances and asked me stay on and make a success of the task.

Once the decision had been taken I plunged wholeheartedly into the preparatory work for ushering in the change in the system, banishing from my mind all the negative thoughts that I had been nurturing.

The change in policy was a thumping success! Far from taking a hit, the revenue actually registered a quantum jump that year!

The wisdom of the representatives of the people had scored over my somewhat bureaucratic resistance.

7. My experiences with Justice Hidayatullah, Vice President of India Acting President?

There is no substitute for patient research and a thorough knowledge of the book of rules - especially while taking a position with superiors.

1982, Shri Giani Zail Singh, the President of India, needed to undergo heart bypass surgery and was to be hospitalized for six weeks. Justice Hidayatullah was the Vice President of India. I was posted as the Secretary to the Vice President, a posting that became a great learning process, providing, as it did a valuable opportunity for close interaction with an eminent jurist and versatile statesman.

Some years prior to that, Justice Hidayatullah was the Chief Justice of India. Shri Neelam Sanjeeva Reddy, the President of India had completed his term and demitted office. Shri V.V. Giri, the then Vice President had resigned from his post to contest the Presidential Election. With the President's position vacant and the Vice President not there, the Chief Justice of India was, in accordance with the provisions of the Constitution of India, sworn in as the acting President. When it was suggested to him that he be described as the "acting" President, he pointed out that the Constitution provides that "there shall be a President of India...", and that he was occupying that post, having resigned from the office of the Chief Justice of India. He was therefore the President of India - not the "acting" President. This position was accepted at that time.

In 1982, as an extension of the earlier precedent, the question was whether we should ask for a seal that read "President of India". I advised him that, this time around, there was a President who only was unable to discharge his functions. The Constitution provides that when the President is unable to discharge his functions the Vice President will do so. Hence the Vice President can only "act" as the President. Advice was sought of Shri Peri Sastry, then the Law Secretary of India, who confirmed the stand I took. The Vice President appreciated the position and possible embarrassment was averted.

8. **Clarity and confidence to the rescue in a delicate situation**

In 1981, as Secretary to the Vice President of India I accompanied Justice Hidayatullah to Canada on an official visit. Dr. Gurdial Singh Dhillion was India's High Commissioner in Canada. Our itinerary took us on a visit to Chateau Montebello, near Quebec, the venue of a recent G7 summit attended among others by Ronald Reagan, (US President), Francois Mitterrand, (French Premier), Pierre Trudeau, (Canadian Prime Minister) and Margaret Thatcher, (British Prime Minister).

En route we were crossing a river on a punt. The High Commissioner walked up to the car in which I was travelling, peeped in and asked "who is the Secretary to the Vice President?" I was in between two other people and raised my hand much like a pupil in a classroom.

"You don't appear to have knowledge of the fundamentals of protocol", he said, and walked away. I jumped out of the car, smoke coming out of my ears, wondering where I had gone wrong. When I asked him what the matter was, Shri Dhillion said that, as I might have noticed, in the carcade from Ottawa to Quebec, his car was trailing the Canadian Protocol Car which, in turn, was behind the Vice President's car. He was agitated that he was unable to fly the Indian flag on his car since the Canadian Protocol vehicle was ahead of his car.

Firmly but very politely, I replied that, while I had a limited knowledge of these matters, there were two things that I wished to point out. Firstly, we were in his jurisdiction - in a country to which he was our High Commissioner - and it was he who put the car plan in place in consultation with the Canadian Government. The Vice President's staff had no role. We simply went by whatever arrangements had been made. Secondly, just as in a parade, (where the parade commander alone salutes, the VIP had the flag, while the rest of the parade comes to attention) in a carcade the leading car, alone, flies the flag; the Vice President's car was flying two flags; as is the custom - Canadian as well as Indian. And that was the correct protocol in my understanding. Shri Dhillion who enjoyed the status and rank of a Cabinet Minister, appeared unconvinced and perhaps protested to the Vice President. That he brought the matter to the notice of the Vice President and reported also to the Government of India, was only made known to me indirectly at a later date. However, I was neither called upon to furnish my explanation subsequently, nor was my understanding of the protocol found fault with.

Sound homework plays an important role in the handling of delicate and sensitive matters. Confidence and clarity of thought are invaluable assets in unforeseen situations.

9. Of Onions and one's Dharma - 1

The Onion crisis in India happened on the verge of the elections in 1996. I was in the Ministry of Agriculture (MoA), as Joint Secretary in charge of Marketing (among other subjects). I was sending daily reports to the Prime Minister's Office (PMO) on the prices of onions in various markets of India, the most important ones being Nasik in Maharashtra and Kamalapuram in Andhra Pradesh.

I asked Shri Kamal Pandey, my mentor and at that time the Agriculture Secretary, Government of India, why we were sending these reports to the PMO. The MoA was in-charge of monitoring the production of commodities, not their sale. Once any produce reaches the farm-gate, it is the job of the Consumer Affairs Department within the Civil Supplies Ministry.

Shri Kamal Pandey asked me whether I intended that he should tell the PMO that he would not send them the reports that they were asking him for! I told him that I was only telling him what our 'Dharma' was as we were doing something not in our line of duty. The information we were gathering may have been inaccurate. And, in the event there was to be an issue about its timeliness or quality, it was going from the wrong source to the PMO. The question was not whether the information should be sent or not, but rather, "who" should send it. I told him that I believed that firstly, every Ministry or Department of the Government of India should do what it is supposed to do, and secondly, it should not do what it is not supposed to do, no matter who is asking you.

A couple of days later Shri Ashok Saikia, a good friend who was a Joint Secretary in the Prime Minister's Office called me. Clearly he was under a lot of pressure at that time. He said "I believe you are having some conscientious objections to the furnishing of this information to the PMO".

I replied that I had no views on the information, per se but only had an issue over the source from which it was being obtained. He was getting impatient, and as I was saying, "Please let me explain...." he hung up saying, "You will explain when your explanation is called for".

No one, however, called for my explanation thereafter. Apparently it was checked up and found that I was right.

In any job, it is very important to know precisely what your functions are, and where your responsibilities do not lie. The system is best served by following it unless, of course, it is changed - which can be done only by those who are in charge of it.

10. Lessons in Dharma - 2

1983 in Andhra Pradesh, Sri N.T. Rama Rao was the new Chief Minister. I was Joint Secretary in the Chief Minister's Office. A resolution had recently been passed by the State Legislative Assembly recommending the abolition of the state Legislative Council (LC). Every LC is constituted through a resolution of the Assembly subsequently approved by Parliament. The Ministry of Home Affairs, Government of India, processes the matter. The same procedure is followed for its abolition.

The budget of the State Government had to be passed. The provisions of the Constitution of India lay down that if a State has two houses, the lower house first passes the budget and the upper house endorses it and returns it. What the upper house says about the budget is not as important as the need for it to consider and return it. While the State Assembly had passed the resolution abolishing the LC the Government of India had not processed its approval yet, thus creating an anomalous situation with reference to the LC in Andhra Pradesh.

Not passing a year's budget had never happened in any State until then. A suggestion was made to promulgate an ordinance, which also would have been an unprecedented step. The Constitutional validity of such a course of action was also not certain.

A financial emergency or the collapse of the constitutional machinery are the two crises no state government wants.

At this point, I made a suggestion to NTR that the practical and constitutionally safe method would be to summon the LC (technically still in existence). The opposition parties may embarrass him by boycotting his call, since his Telugu Desam Party (TDP) had no members in the LC yet. I pointed out, that the numbers of the Assembly were such that TDP could have nine members in the LC, and nine was the quorum of the LC. Surely, the nine TDP members, (who needed to be nominated yet, and would be members only for a short while until Parliament approved the proposal for abolition of the LC), would attend the LC. When the budget was tabled in the LC, that house would be formally in order in terms of the requirement of quorum. Because of the lack of majority the budget would not be endorsed, but that was not necessary. The LC only needed to consider and return the budget to the Assembly. Thus was passed the Budget of Andhra Pradesh in 1983.

A possible emergency in the State was avoided by using the extant law and procedures although the solution may not have been politically palatable.

11. The "birdie" and the Vice President

I was Secretary to the Governor of Andhra Pradesh when Smt. Sharda Mukherjee was the Governor.She had very cordial relations with Vice President Justice Hidayatullah's family. Aftermoving over to Gujarat as the Governor of the state, she visited Vice President Hidayatullah's office while on a visit to Delhi. She apparently advised Justice Hidayatullah that he would find a young IAS officer of great help in organizing his office a little more systematically than it was at that time. She then suggested my name which the Vice President passed on to the Government of India.The appointment was made shortly thereafter.

Apart from being Chairman ex officio of the Rajya Sabha in Parliament, the Vice President has many functions including attendance at ceremonial and formal occasions involving elaborate protocol.Apart from ministerial staff, his secretariat comprises a complement of security and personal staff, some drawn from the Rajya Sabha Secretariat.

Though I was a relatively junior officer of the rank of a Director in the Government of India, the position enjoyed the rank of a head of the department.

In addition to being the head of the secretariat, my duties entailed accompanying the Vice President whenever he so desired. One ground rule I had laid down with the VP's approval was that, unlike his personal staff I would go only to places where I was also invited separately. This applied also to the national days of various countries to the functions organized for the celebration of which the VP invariably was the Chief Guest.

It would normally have been part of my duties to gather material for the VP's use in the making of speeches. In Justice

Hidayatullah's case, however, I was rarely called up on to do so as he was a learned person and a consummate speaker.

Justice Hidayatullah regularly played golf at the course in Rashtrapathi Bhavan mainly with the Military Staff of the President. On one occasion he scored a "birdie" (one stroke under par for a hole) generally regarded as a significant achievement in amateur golf. As is customary on such occasions the other players arrange a dinner at Rashtrapathi Bhavan in his honour. As he was leaving, the VP indicated that he was expecting me to join him. I explained to him that it was, firstly, a private occasion and that, in any case, I had not been invited. He felt, momentarily, that perhaps I was standing on undue formality. He did not however stress the matter and proceeded for the dinner though perhaps somewhat unhappy at my attitude.

The point here was that I had a duty to preserve the distinction between the duties of his personal staff and those who were part of his Secretariat - duties which, admittedly, were very much in the process of being defined for the first time after many decades.

I felt it important that, at that sensitive stage, when the nature of the duties of the staff was being spelt out, such nuances had to be recognized and their implications clearly dealt with.

Justice Hidayatullah was a person with vast public experience, sensitive to the feelings of other people and broad minded in his approach. Once the point had been made he went along with the logic of it and things soon settled down to a satisfactory rhythm.

12. Individual Excellence vis a vis the safety of group effort

In the year 1997, Shri Kamal Pandey was the Secretary of the Department of Agriculture and Cooperation (DOAC) in the Ministry of Agriculture, Government of Indiaand I was serving as a Joint Secretary in that Ministry. Among other subjects, I was handling Policy Planning and was charged with instituting innovative and contemporary methods of dealing with issues which the ministry was concerned with. Naturally some of the initiatives questioned the basis of established and time-tested approaches, and methods, changing which met with expected resistance.

Making the annual forecast for the food production of the country was an important function of the DOAC- a responsibility entrusted to the Economic and Statistical Advisor (ESA). Shri Pandey and I discussed with Dr. G.S. Ram, the then ESA, the desirability of altering the structure of the methodology followed in making the forecast. The extent practice was to consolidate estimates obtained periodically from the various States and Union Territories of the country. The primary estimates were generated by the Economics and Statics departmentsof the states/UTs which were based on the conduct of crop cutting experiments for different crops in the Kharif and Rabi seasons I felt that this approach could be substantially refined by infusing into it the principles of modern tools such as the discipline of Econometrics and the technique of Crop Modelling. Dr. Ram was reluctant to embark up on what he felt was needless tinkering with a method that had proved adequate until then. On my initiative the Secretary prevailed up on the ESA to adopt the new approach.

A forecast was accordingly produced - showing a likely deficit of about three million tonnes of wheat in that year compared with the known requirement. This fact was brought to the notice of the Ministry of Food and was placed before the Union Cabinet, which decided to import the said quantity of wheat.The responsibility was entrusted to the Ministry of Commerce which, in turn, gave the job to the State Trading Corporation of India (STC).An Argentinian private company won the tenders floated by STC.

The wheat supplied, however, was upon inspection at the time of import, foundto be infected by a pest. Most of the northern and western regions of the country are wheat producing areas and wheat is not widely consumed in the south or east. It was therefore decided not to discharge the wheat in to the market. As a result it was lying in the godowns at the port of import. Overtime, the wheat began to rot. The issue was raised in Parliament, and not surprisingly, an inquiry ordered into the matter - to be conducted by the Central Bureau of Investigation (CBI). And the first thing that investigating agency wished to know, upon commencement of the investigation, was the identity of the person/agency that putout the estimate in the first place!

Clearly not only was Dr. Ram in a potentially difficult situation but also it was I who landed him there. While nothing untoward eventually ensued, the relative safety - of the consolidation of a large number reports received from various sources at several times- vis a vis the application on the part of individual of his expertise to the exercise was brought out vividly!

There is a feeling, especially in the middle rungs of administration, that accountability is transiting from being a requirement to becoming an obsession. While it is a most desirable and forward looking step, the coming into being of a new ethic of accountability following the enactment of the Right to Information Act has brought with it the need to ensure that the ability to perform on the part of individuals and agencies is not unduly compromised on account of apprehensions caused the raised bar of accountability.

Like in many other areas of public administration the two compulsions, both equally important, namely the freedom to act in good faith without fear of being needlessly found fault with and the need to remain accountable for one's actions - have to be harmonised. Else, the integrity of the ambience pervading the apparatus of governance can be adversely impacted. This can cause conflict and doubt in the minds of those tasked with sensitive functions involving use of the discretion and individual analytical skills.

Unless this balance is brought about, the imperatives of excellence in performance and compliance with the demand for accountability can act at cross purposes and prove unproductive in the long run.

13. The Importance of understanding the principles of social cost benefit

The stint I had as the Managing Director of the Andhra Pradesh Fisheries Development Corporation (APFDC), was probably the most satisfying posting I had.

I was, in 1979, posted as the Managing Director of APFDC a public sector undertaking of the Andhra Pradesh government which was entrusted several functions relating to the fisheries sector. These include the operation of fishing trawlers, running an ice plant and a prawn processing unit, construction of trawlers in a shipyard and the procurement and sale of fresh water and marine prawns and fish from the operators of mechanized fishing boats operating from the fishing harbors along the cost of the state and from individual fishermen fishing with traditional craft and tackle.

The prospect of being able to contribute to the economic well-being of the traditional fishermen and promoting consumption of fish especially by the inmates of the hostels meant for school and college students belonging to the Schedule Castes, Schedule Tribes and Backward Castes excited me the most. The fishermen inhabiting villages lying along the coast constitute a community that is geographically isolated and excluded from many of the advantages those inland take for granted. The occupation is risky, hazardous and seasonal. Levels of illiteracy and superstition are high. Access to basic minimum needs including drinking water, housing, power, education and health is far less compared to other sections of the population. Needless to say the fishermen are exposed probably to the highest degree of exploitation especially on account of his livelihood depending upon marketing of a of a highly perishable commodity.

As soon as the Catamaran lands the fishermen have, literally within minutes, to dispose of his catch accepting the best possible price offered to him by the merchant. This is because the individual fisherman has no means of access to insulated transport, cold storage and he is unable to demand or obtain a fair price for his commodity and is left at the mercy of the middle man.

Unfortunately the Fishermen Cooperative Societies formed with a view to strengthening the working capital base of the fishermen and providing them the economies of the scale necessary for the establishment of, and ensuring access to, infrastructure facilities such as storage and transport, were a story of failure – once again on account of sabotage on the part of those who stood to lose if the Societies had succeeded in achieving their objectives.

I sensed a great opportunity in the situation. APFDC had the wherewithal to own or operate the necessary infrastructure and provide access thereto to the fishermen. By establishing a sequence of simple linkages the landings of the fishermen could be connected to the best possible markets, and the individual fisherman's share in the consumer - rupee enhanced substantially, even after allowing for a reasonable commission for the Corporations to cover its expenditure.

Accordingly a scheme (which had been already formulated but not implemented yet) for internal marketing of marine fish was operationalized. A string of outlets was opened along the coast. Fish catches were procured, loaded on to insulated vans transported to the nearest consumption centres and marketed at a price which was passed on to the fishermen deducting a margin enough to cover the corporations expenses.

As expected the arrangement resulted in fishermen securing, on an average, a rupee (in those days) per kg of fish, more than what the merchants were offering. The merchants, naturally refused to be pushed out of their traditional business. They responded by raising the prices offered by them for different varieties of fish, in order to keep their supply chain intact. This, in fact, was what we wanted in APFDC!

Overtime the outlets continued with APFDC's presence acting as insurance and securing for the fishermen a consistently higher price from the middle man. In the process, naturally, purchases and sale by the APFDC dwindled, and after sometime ground to a halt. While this posed no problem to the fishermen, the finance department of the state government which had sanctioned the project on the assurance by the APFDC that the margins realized from the operations at a certain level would ensure that the activity was financially viable, noticed that losses weremounting steadily as commitments on account of the staff and infrastructure continued although the transactions had stopped. The state government promptly asked APFDC to discontinue the operations!

A closer look at the seemingly ambiguous situation could have revealed that what appeared to be an apparent loss was actually the sum that represented the additional income accruing to the fishermen. Merely by being present at the market place APFDC was able to ensure to the fishermen an income much higher than what they would have earned in its absence. In the long run, a higher level of economic wellbeing of the fishermen community, should normally have led to a reduction in the commitment, on the part of the government, to that community in terms of supply of subsidized food, provision of scholarships in schools, an free medical facilities in hospitals and such measures meant for the people living below the poverty line - a line the fishermen would hopefully have crossed.

This however, was not an approach which was an integral part of appraising the soundness of socio economic initiatives, at least in those days.

Just as in the case of activities of other public sector undertakings it is necessary that consideration of social cost benefit inform, the exercises evaluating the efficacy of initiatives undertaken.

14. General Thimmayya's cap

Historically few institutions have valued the importance of established protocols and standard operating procedures so much as the Armed Forces. Running through a checklist is nothing new today for professionals such as a pilot commencing a flight or a surgeon beginning an operation.A probably apocryphal story concerning the legendary India Chief of Army Staff General Cariappa and his Deputy, General Thimmayya illustrates the case in point in a rather light hearted vein.

General Thimmayya had an appointment with his Chief for a drink at 7.00 pm on a given day. That the two Generals were cousins obviously had no bearing on the formality attached to the occasion and the rigour demanded in terms of preparation for it. Thimmayya spent a whole week - assiduously polishing the brass, shining shoes and ironing the uniform. The distance to the Chief's house was measured as was the travel time.

On the appointed day General Thimmayya arrived, as planned, a few minutes in advance at the entrance to the Chief's house. He waited till the time was right, drove in, stepped out the car and executed a perfectly practiced smart salute and said "Good evening Sir!"

General Cariappa's response was, "Timmy, where is your cap"?

Apparently, absorbed as he was in the thoroughness of preparation for the occasion, General Thimmayya had overlooked the most important item of his attire – the cap!

Such, then, is the need for ensuring that the requisite level of preparedness for any important task should be broken down into the small but important steps that comprise that exercise and followed meticulously. The confidence and assurance that result from the knowledge that preparation was complete and comprehensive, always adds great value to performance.

15. The Directors Interview

It was the year 1968, and I had joined for training as an IAS probationer in the Lal Bahadur Shastri National Academy of Administration (as it is now known), Mussoorie. The Director of the Academy at that time was Shri K.K. Das a very senior, highly respected and distinguished Civil Servant.

As was the custom the Director had lined up a series of interviews with the trainees partly in order to get to know them better individually, as also to infuse in them a sense of confidence of comfort about what was in store.

My own slot was at 3.00 pm on a particular day.

I was playing bridge in a colleague's room, when I suddenly realised that it was time for my appointment.

I had barely fifteen minutes within which to run to my room, dress and sprint to the Director's Chambers. Those familiar with the terrain of hill stations will understand how much of effort is required to do all this when everything is either up there or down there.

I ran all the way up to the Director's room and entered – a few minutes late, somewhat flustered, huffing and puffing. Guiltily I conjured up the excuse of an upset stomach as the cause for my being late. Unfortunately the matter did not end there and the Director promptly asked what medication I was having. Unprepared as I was for this affected solicitude and detailed interrogation; I concocted an explanation that it was a homeopathic remedy. Much to my chagrin the proceedings continued. "Ah!. And what may the remedy be"? continued the Director. Adlibbing uncontrollably by now, I said "Something my mother gave me Sir. I do not really know the name."The cat was out of the bag. The Director abandoned the inquisition with a knowing smile. I still wake up at night sweating at the memory of the close escape.

The moral of the story? The truth is the safest bet in a crisis as the alternative invariably plunges one into the morasse of a downward spiral of fiction which cannot face more than skin - deep interrogation

16. Systems and Transparency vis a vis subjectivity

One learns from experience that while transparency is desirable, it has to be practiced with an eye on striking the proper balance between objectivity and the value of subjective judgement.

Consider for instance, the recruitment practices of the Union Public Service Commission of India (UPSC).Candidates need not merely to demonstrate the extent of their knowledge but have also display personality skills. The recruitment is thus adequately transparent but tempered with a modicum of the all-important human element which is essentially subjective in nature.

Totally mechanical approaches are often more suitable for exercises not influenced by the unpredictability associated with the behavior of human beings.

In the year 1984 I served (as the Registrar of Co-operative Societies) on a Committee tasked with re-organizing the geographical jurisdiction of Primary of Agricultural Co-operative Societies (PACSs) in the erstwhile state of Andhra Pradesh. PACSs were classified as viable, potentially viable or unviable depending on the excess of income over expenditure. In accordance with regulations then in force of the Reserve Bank of India, the interest due on the loans outstanding of a PACS was the primary consideration for determining income. This time, however, the Committee enlarged the scope of the definition by introducing some more factors relating to the operational viability of a society -such as the presence of non-loanee farmers in its area operations, the extent of cropped land yet to be covered by lending, the potential for creating irrigation facilities, the presence of infrastructure such as power supply, etc. Different weightages were assigned to the various parameters in accordance with their perceived *inter se* significance and scores allotted to the parameters. Cut off points were prescribed for societies to be as considered viable - which varied across different parts of the state depending on levels of economic development and the agro - ecological conditions.

Marks were then awarded to each society and recommendations made whether the society was to be divided, left intact or merged with another, so that the resultant society would be a viable one.

When the process was completed the total number of societies which was initially 6785 as on 30th June, 1987 came down to 4630 as on 30th June, 1989. The village co-operative in those days commanded considerable economic resources and political importance. The process resulted in a great deal of litigation and the Department of Cooperation had to defend its decisions in hundreds of cases filed in courts of law. Owing to the pains taken to render the process rational and transparent, and also on account of the availability of computerized records that justified the ultimate decision most of the cases were decided in favour of the Department.

In the aforementioned case a transparent and methodical approach served to aid rational decision making which stood up to external scrutiny.

In another instance that supports the case inpoint, one of my colleagues, as the Chairman of a major public sector Colliery, made aspirants competing for selection as security guards participate in a sprint. Those who ran the fastest were selected! Physical fitness and stamina being the essential requisites for that selection, the method followed eliminated the scope of outside interference.

This was not so, however, in the case of the procedure adopted by another colleague who headed the Department of

Agriculture in the erstwhile State of Andhra Pradesh. A large number of posts of Assistant Agricultural Officers had to be filled. Applications were called for. Based on the details available in the application forms, marks were given for different aspects of the applicants' background such as academic qualifications, previous experience, proficiency in the official language, etc. The posts were filled entirely on the basis of the marks scored. Calling the candidates for interviews would no doubt have exposed the exercise to outside interference. Still, while eliminating the subjective element no doubt insulated the process from external factors, one would still liked to see an effort made to assess the personalities of the candidates before selection, as this was important having regard to of the nature of duties they were expected to perform after selection.

Thus, while objective criteria have their value in aiding decision-making, the need for infusing in element of judgment should be kept in mind when the context is appropriate.

As always, it is a question of balance.

17. Prevention of corruption - the need for a mature and balanced approach

Good governance has for several decades figured high on the agenda of the National and State Governments in our country.

Corruption, nepotism, leakages and incompetence are among the many scourges that have tainted the image of, and adversely affected, the performance of the administrations at various levels. As always, the worst sufferers have been the public at large - especially the poor and the excluded sections thereof.

It is not my intention here to discuss different aspects of the malaise of corruption-its causes, the common forms in which it presents itself, or the most effective methods of containing it. The point I wish to make is that in its essential form, it is the reflection of generic weaknesses germane to the socio-economic structure and the set of rewards/punishments established by that structure.

I was the sub-collector of Ongole revenue division in Prakasam district of the erstwhile Andhra Pradesh state in 1971.There was a prolonged dry spell causing acute distress to the agriculture sector, especially the agricultural labour and small/marginal farmers. As a measure of succour to the affected people the government announced grant of distress taccavi loans (as they were then known in those parts) – which were essentially consumption loans meant to mitigate the loss of livelihoods on account of drought conditions.

In order to eliminate possible malpractices by the officials at the village, firka (group of villages) and taluka levels, the government instructed the revenue divisional officers to undertake disbursement of the loans in person. I accordingly carried cash and distributed Rs. 50/- each to 300 beneficiaries in one village.

Upon my return to headquarters late in the evening I received a message that, after my departure from the village, the beneficiaries queued up in front of the residences of the village officers and voluntarily paid them Rs. 5/- per head. I was naturally furious. Upon mature reflection, however, I realized that the residents of the village needed to maintain harmony in their relationship with the village officers who were a permanent part of the socio-economic structure of the village. I, as the divisional officer, was perceived as a one-off and short lived external intervention. Also, there was neither a demand for the sum the beneficiaries parted with nor was any favour promised or done in return. I could have booked criminal cases under the Prevention of Corruption Act against those who paid the money as well as the village officers. I desisted however, as such a step would, in the circumstances, be seen as an overreaction not serving any significant purpose.

A sense of proportion and balance needs to inform the approach to corruption. While the malady ought not to be countenanced in any form or degree, it is easy to miss the wood for the tree if one lacks the ability to ignore the trivial. As I have discussed elsewhere in this book, preoccupation with what can be ignored can adversely impact on the time and energy available to address larger issues.

18. Cracking the whip: when authority conquered anarchy

While arriving at a set of priorities is important for one to be an effective team leader, it is equally necessary to be able to convey those priorities to the members of the team, as well as those whom the team exists to serve. It is often essential to send the right signals out by setting an example by one's actions.

In 1972, there was a prolonged and widespread public agitation in the Andhra region of the erstwhile Andhra Pradesh state. The demand was for a separate Andhra state.

Those in authority, as well as prominent leaders of the movement, became helpless spectators as the movement escalated. They wanted to achieve amity politically by allowing tempers to cool. For too long, they desisted from stern action against the agitators who were emotionally charged. Such was this spontaneity of the public sentiment at that time that, no sooner than someone called for a stoppage (bundh) of work, everyone responded without so much as ascertaining the legitimacy of the source of the announcement. This happened frequently and government offices, business establishments and educational institutions alike remained shut down for several months at a stretch throughout that region.

The agitation witnessed several violent incidents all over the state. On several occasions the uprisal had to be quelled with measures such as lathi charges, the use of tear gas shells and even firing. Unlawful elements often exploited the situation with the innocent public suffering the consequences.

When things got out of hand at a point, the central government stepped in. The popularly elected Legislative Assembly was dissolved, the Council of Ministers asked to resign and President's rule imposed. The Governor along with his Advisers took over the reigns of the government which now comprised only of officials.

I was serving as the sub-collector of Ongole revenue division in Prakasam district at that time.

On the 22nd of November, 1972 the police in Ongole town had to resort to lathi-charge, and tear-gas to disburse a crowd of agitators. When those measures failed, they opened fire killing four people. Curfew was imposed in the town and shoot-at-sight orders enforced.

I was camping in the nearby Chirala town at that time. In the wake of the incident the Collector summoned me back to Ongole. As I was entering the town I could see flames rising into the sky as several building were burning, having been set afire by the angry mob fleeing from the place of the incident. A group of agitating youth stopped me from entering the town as they felt that my presence would strengthen the hands of the official machinery. It was only after patiently persuading them that I would have a constructive role to play in restoring peace and order in the town that I was allowed to enter. The Collector, the Superintendent of Police and I discussed in detail the measures to bring t he situation under control quickly.

Quite obviously the administration had lost its connect with the people who were angry and upset. None was willing to participate in any discussions. Several attempts to bring to the table prominent citizens who could assist in the process were of to no avail. The situation clearly called for some out-of-the-box thinking.

The Superintendent of Police and I hit upon a bright idea. Shri Karavadi Venkateswarulu was a well-known lawyer and known to be of socialistic persuasion. I had cordial relations with him and he enjoyed considerable goodwill with the citizens of the town. Deliberately, we had him picked up and kept in detention overnight. That action was both legally permissible as possible to defend under the circumstances. The move outraged the city community with both the youth and the elders expressing dismay at the turn of events. Several leading citizens sought a meeting with us the next morning. This gave us the opportunity we wanted to re-establish a rapport with the people. Naturally we retraced the step of detaining Shri Venkateswarulu. But in the process we managed to secure the cooperation of the leaders to form a Peace Committee to oversee the measures to restore normalcy and create in the minds of people a sense of confidence and trust in the administration.

The very next day there was an abrupt deterioration in the law and order situation in Chirala town. The force earlier available there had returned along with me to Ongole the previous day. Chirala had, in fact, being the more sensitive of the two towns and witness to many major incidents in the past. In the aftermath of the Ongole incident an enraged mob attacked the police station and was fired upon. Fortunately the situation was quickly brought under control.

Barring these two unfortunate events Prakasam district remained generally peaceful. The agitation, however, continued elsewhere in the state.

Overtime, with the central government remaining firm in its opposition to the demand of the separatists, enthusiasm flagged and public support dwindled. The employees of the government and those in the private sector had to borrow in order to survive. The resources available with those supporting the movement from behind the scenes also dried up and the agitation petered out.

Traders and business establishments opened shop once again.

Government employees called off the strike. Public utilities began to function normally. Private and public transport services resumed. One was finally able to breathe freely and think of matters other than maintaining law and order.

The return to normalcy was, however, a slow process. The administration which had been in slumber for several months, was limping back to the performance of its regular functions in a very tardy manner.

The government directed all the Departments and their functionaries at various levels to take steps to ensure that its presence of was felt by the public. Several regulatory measures were set in motion. The staff of the municipalities of the cities commenced checking the quality of food stuffs in hotels and restaurants. The Department of Legal Metrology began check to the weights and measures used by traders. Engineers of the Irrigation and Power Departments moved around to ensure that the infrastructure was intact and canals, electric lines transformers and power stations were property maintained.

In the rural areas, we felt that collecting paddy from the farmers towards what was known as the Producers' Levy would be a good entry point for the exercise. The system in the state of Andhra Pradesh at that time was (and continues to be now in the states of Andhra Pradesh and Telangana) that rice was normally procured from the rice millers who, in turn, purchased paddy from the farmers. The millers milled the paddy and sold the rice to the Food Corporation of India (FCI) which was the agent of the State Government for collecting and storing rice. This time around, however, we felt that procurement of paddy directly from the farmers (as is the normal practice in States such as Uttarakhand, Haryana and Punjab in the case of wheat) would have a more telling impact. And we did this under the provisions of the Defence of India rules then in force, more for the dramatic effect than on account of the lack of statutory authority.

In one prosperous village a very well to do farmer was identified. He was a person who, even at the peak of the agitation, had remained on good terms with the administration. I had been in frequent touch with him to preserve an ear to the ground at a time when traditional sources of information were not available. We had information that he had stored a large amount of paddy out of which the levy due would be substantial. When he wavered in compliance, the FCI moved in and forcibly took possession of the paddy. The news of the incident spread like wild fire all over the district and large quantities of paddy began to flow into the godowns without our having resort to any coercion. The status of the individual chosen, as well as his known proximity with the administration, together with the repercussions of that followed his non-cooperation, had the desired impact.

We next turned our attention to Singarayakonda, a busy little town straddled by the national highway from Chennai to Kolkata passing through the District. There were a large number of encroachments on both sides of the road, many of which had sprung up recently owing largely to the fact that administration had been sluggish for a long time. As a part of the strategy to convey to the public the determination of the government to enforce regulations, we decided to free the town of the encroachments. Once again, we took care to choose large areas occupied unlawfully by prominent establishments like a movie theatre and a hotel. Notices ordering the removal of the structures within 24 hours were served upon them– late on a Friday evening, making it difficult, if not impossible, for the parties to secure stay orders from courts of law. The very next day a large contingent of labour, equipped with the necessary tools, was moved in and the encroachments forcibly removed, literally overnight. The suddenness of the action and the freeing of an important communication artery from the clogging caused by the encroachments, together with the factor of visibility that came with the identity of encroachers, mode a substantial impact on the residents of the town.

These exemplary actions, among many others, contributed in a large measure to the success of the effort or reviving the image of the administrative machinery and in invoking in the public mind a sense of respect for the authority of the government that had for long been allowed to fall into disuse.

5.2 Illustrative Cases

CASE 1

The Issue:

You have been working with your team for almost a year. One of your subordinates Mr. A is very effective and hardworking; he takes responsibility and gets things done. However, you have heard that Mr. A makes loose comments about women. Mrs. X who is working under A, comes to you, she is visibly disturbed. She tells you that Mr. A has been making undue advances towards her and has even asked her to go out for dinner with him. She wants to give a written complaint seeking action against Mr. A. what would you do and why?

Recommended Approach

Such alleged improper, if not indecent, behaviour with women cannot be countenanced, no matter whatever be the circumstances. However, A is a valued asset to the orgnisation. Since his version of the story is yet unknown. It would therefore be desirable, as a first step, to call him and let him know of the complaint – (without divulging the identity of Mrs. X to avoid possible embarrassment).

If A denies the allegations, the only option is to force a face-off between the two and forward the compliant to the internal complaints committee to decide whose version is correct and proceed to terminate the services of the guilty.

If, on the other hand, A confesses to his guilt, I will administer a stern warning to him, ask him to apologise to Mrs. X and also commit him to avoiding recurrence of such incidents in the future. In addition disciplinary action will lie against A.

CASE 2

The Issue:

You have grown up with X, who has been your best friend since childhood. You have shared your joys and sorrows and have been each other's confidante. Both of you are in your final year graduation and writing your final exams. In the exam you notice that your friend is copying and cheating a lot. What would you do and why?

Recommended Approach

Clearly, cheating is unacceptable and I cannot be a party to its continuance. On the other hand, X is a friend and causing him harm in any way would be the last thing I would want.

Detecting cheating and proceeding against the offenders is the duty of the invigilating staff and not my responsibility. Therefore after the examination is over I would clearly state that I disapprove of his conduct and chose not to complaint against him on account of our friendship. If, however, he does not desist from cheating in the future, I will be forced to bring the matter to the notice of those concerned, our relationship notwithstanding.

CASE 3

The Issue:

You are posted as the Medical Superintendent of a District level Govt. Hospital which caters to the needs of poor patients from surrounding rural areas along with the local people from the district town. As such the hospital has very good infrastructure and adequate equipment to cater to this need. It also receives sufficient funds to meet the recurring expenditure. In spite of this there have been repeated complaints particularly from the patients which include the following:

(i) Very poor maintenance and unhygienic conditions in hospital premises.

(ii) The hospital staff frequently demanding bribes from the patients for the services rendered.

(iii) The negligent attitude of the doctors resulting in casualities at times.

(iv) Siphoning of a substantial stock of medicine by the staff and selling it out.

(v) Strong nexus between the senior doctors of the hospital and the owners of local private nursing homes and testing labs as a result of which the patients are strongly misled and dissuaded from availing the hospital facilities and rather compelled to purchase costly medicines from market and get medical tests and even operations done at private medical houses.

(vi) There also exist notorious employee unions which put undue pressure and resent any reformative step by the administration. Ponder over the situation and suggest effective ways to tackle each of the above mentioned problems.

Recommended Approach

A holistic approach is needed to deal with such a situation. Transparency and accountability in the conduct of the staff and creation of awareness on the part of the patients should be the hallmarks of an improved atmosphere brought about by a carrot and stick policy - involving both immediate responses and long term measures.

(i) Firstly, cleanliness being an overriding priority in a hospital, a proper incentive structure should be put in place to encourage healthy competition amongst the units of the hospital and employees to reward, both monetarily and otherwise, the maintenance of the highest levels of hygiene.

(ii) Patients are the most important stakeholders of the hospital. They should be made aware of their rights and encouraged to bring to the notice of the authorities any improper activity on the part of the doctors or staff. I will make myself easily accessible to the patients, in addition to being prompt and effective in dealing with their grievances. Frequent meetings will be held with the patients or their representatives to ascertain their complaints. Strict and speedy action will be taken against persons found guilty, after due enquiry - especially the senior most staff - in order to send a proper signal to the environment.

(iii) The entire system of stocking and distribution of medicines will be automated urgently, with built in checks, to avoid recurrence of shortages or pilferage.

(iv) Establishment of standard protocols for laboratory tests as well as surgeries and ensuring adherence to them by the doctors and technicians will be given the highest priority and the patients made aware of the steps taken.

(v) I will also hold consultations with the doctors and other employees to create a disciplined and efficient atmosphere in the organization. Frequent surprise checks will be conducted and deficiencies and misconduct firmly dealt with.

(vi) To break the nexus between the employees and private nursing homes, strict action will be taken in a few select cases, preferably against senior functionaries to send a clear message to the organization that the administration will not tolerate such activities.

(vii) Simultaneously, every effort will be made, in an inclusive and participatory manner, to address the genuine grievances of the employees, create an espirit de crops and improve the work ethic and enhance the commitment to the cause of providing better services. Identification of some employees as change-agents and provision of encouragement to them will be undertaken, side by side, as a part of improvement process, initiating proceedings against those who refuse to adhere to the systems introduced.

(viii) This holistic and multi-pronged strategy will be incorporated in the hospitals "Citizen's Charter" and monitored closely against a set of deliverables over pre-determined time lines. Assistance of an external consultant will be secured to perform the task.

(ix) While this exercise is on I will also maintain a close liaison with the Labour Department to guard against any organized resistance by the workers.

CASE 4

The Issue:

Sivakasi in Tamil Nadu is known for its manufacturing clusters on firecrackers and matches. The local economy of the area is largely dependent on firecrackers industry. It has led to tangible economic development and improved standard of living in the area.

So far as child labour norms for hazardous industries such as fire crackers industry are concerned, the International Labour Organization (ILO) has set the minimum age as 18 years. In India, however, this age is 14 years.

The units in industrial clusters of firecrackers can be classified into registered and non-registered entities. One typical unit is household-based work. Though the law is clear on the use of child labour employment norms in registered/ non-registered units, it does not include household-based works. Household-based work means children working under the supervision of their parents/relatives. To evade child labour norms, several units project themselves as household-based works but employ children from outside. Needless to say that employing children saves the costs for these units leading to higher profits to the owners.

On your visit to one of the units at Sivakasi, the owner takes you around the unit which has about 10-15 children below 14 years of age. The owner tells you that in his household-based unit, the children are all his relatives. You notice that several children smirk, when the owner tells you this. On deeper enquiry, you figure out that neither the owner nor the children are able to satisfactorily establish their relationship with each other. Bring out and discuss the ethical issues involved in the above cases.

Recommended Approach

The only ethical issue involved in the case is the menace of poverty and finding a way to save the children from this menace. The rights of the children have to be protected and at the same time care has to be taken of the fact that the children are able to survive this menace.

The immediate action that I will take will be to order the closure of the errant factories. The children belong to the poor background and stopping them from work will escalate their difficulties. To take care of this, I will also look for ways for the rehabilitation of the children.

I will also order action against the erring unit and the employer and proprietor of the unit for employing child labour. The action will serve as a deterrent for the other units operating in the area to mend their ways. At the same time a notice will be sent to all the other units and an enquiry will be conducted against them.

The different institutes of the state and the NGOs which work in these areas will be contacted and their services will be used for the rehabilitation of the children. There are also different schemes and acts (the most notable being the Right to Education Act) of the government in areas of child education and welfare, I will also look at the eligibility criteria to avail the benefits under those schemes and try to bring the eligible children under the umbrella of those schemes/benefits.

CASE 5

The Issue:

A Public Information Officer has received an application under RTI Act. Having gathered the information, the PIO discovers that the information pertains to some of the decisions taken by him, which were found to be not altogether right. There were other employees also who were party to these decisions. Disclosure of the information is likely to lead to disciplinary action with possibility of punishment against him as well as some of his colleagues. Non-disclosure or part disclosure or camouflaged disclosure of information will result into lesser punishment or no punishment.

The PIO is otherwise an honest and conscientious person but this particular decision, on which the RTI application has been filed, turned out to be wrong. He comes to you for advice. Please indicate what you would like to advice, giving proper reasons.

Recommended Approach

It is very necessary to look into certain attributes of any decision making process before declaring it right or wrong. The three attributes are whether the decision taken is arbitrary, whether it is taken with malafide intentions and whether it is discriminatory. If any of these three attributes are present in a decision, then it is a colored exercise of decision.

Under the RTI act, it is the constitutional duty of the State to provide information unless, the information asked for is exempted by the Act. I will see whether the information asked for comes under that exemption or not. If it does not, then I will tell the PIO that he has to furnish information because suppressing it will be illegal. I will also advise him to keep in picture his immediate superior officer and have his support in case of any repercussions.

CASE 6

The Issue:

You are working as an Executive Engineer in the construction cell of a Municipal Corporation and are presently in-charge of the construction of a flyover. There are two Junior Engineers under you who have the responsibility of day-to-day inspection of the site and are reporting to you, while you are finally reporting to the Chief Engineer who heads the cell. While the construction is heading towards completion, the Junior Engineers have been regularly reporting that all construction is taking place as per design specifications. However, in one of your surprise inspections, you have noticed some serious deviations and lacunae which, in your opinion, are likely to affect the safety of the flyover. Rectification of these lacunae at this stage would require a substantial amount of demolition and rework which will cause a tangible loss to the contractor and will also delay completion. There is a lot of public pressure on the Corporation to get this construction completed because of heavy traffic congestion in the area. When you brought this matter to the notice of the Chief Engineer, he advised you that in his opinion it is not a very serious lapse and may be ignored. He further advised for expediting the project for completion in time. However, you are convinced that this was a serious matter which might affect public safety and should not be left unaddressed.

What will you do in such a situation? Suggest what course of action you would like to take, giving reasons.

Recommended Approach

I will prepare a detailed report of the situation with all the facts and my analysis and present it to the Chief Engineer. I will request him to study my report and take a decision. Based on his decision in a written communication, I will take the further course of action.

If in his reply the Chief Engineer wants to continue the project then I will act accordingly. As the Chief Engineer is a person with greater experience and if in his opinion the lapse is not very serious, I need to respect his opinion.

CASE 7

The Issue:

You are heading a leading technical institute of the country. The institute is planning to convene an interview panel shortly under your chairmanship for selection of the post of professors. A few days before the interview, you get a call from the Personal Secretary (PS) of a senior government functionary seeking your intervention in favour of the selection of a close relative of the functionary for this post. The PS also informs you that he is aware of the long pending and urgent proposals of your institute for grant of funds for modernization, which are awaiting the functionary's approval. He assures you that he would get these proposals cleared.

What are the options available to you? Evaluate each of these options and choose the option which you would adopt, giving reasons.

Recommended Approach

Heading a leading technical institute of the country is in itself an honor that has been provided to somebody in the wake of his/her achievements in life. It is not unusual to receive such calls from various quarters seeking favors. The imperatives of integrity and ethics and the need to protect the dignity of the office will have to guide my decision, apart from being true to myself and judging the candidate on his merits and not by any other considerations.

CASE 8

The Issue:

As a senior officer in the Finance Ministry, you have access to some confidential and crucial information about policy decisions that the Government is about to announce. These decisions are likely to have far-reaching impact on the housing and construction industry. If the builders have access to this information beforehand, they can make huge profits. One of the builders has done a lot of quality work for the Government and is known to be close to your immediate superior, who asks you to disclose this information to the said builder.

Recommended Approach

As a senior officer of a central ministry, one is bound by the code of conduct of that particular organization and if certain information is confidential, it is supposed to be kept so regardless of the pressure being applied. It would be totally unethical and a breach of the code of conduct to divulge such details to anyone.

Therefore, I will refuse to furnish the information to the builder, after explaining the position firmly but politely to my superior.

CASE 9

The Issue:

You are the Executive Director of an upcoming InfoTech Company which is making a name for itself in the market. Mr. A, who is a star performer, is heading the marketing team. In a short period of one year, he has helped in doubling the revenues as well as creating high brand equity for the Company so much so that you are thinking of promoting him. However, you have been receiving information from many corners about his attitude towards the female colleagues; particularly his habit of making loose comments on women. In addition, he regularly sends indecent SMS's to all the team members including his female colleagues. One day, late in the evening, Mrs. X, who is one of Mr. A's team members, comes to you visibly disturbed. She complains against the continued misconduct of Mr. A, who has been making undesirable advances towards her and has even tried to touch her inappropriately in his cabin. She tenders her resignation and leaves your office.

Recommended Approach

The first and foremost step would be to make sure that the female employee is heard properly. All efforts will be made to make sure that she realizes that the organisation is with her and every step will be taken to ensure that justice is done to her. The next step would be to order an enquiry by the Internal Sexual Harassment Committee in accordance with the provisions of the Sexual Harassment of Women at Workplace (Prevention, Prohibition and Redressal) Act, 2013. If the charges are found to be true, the matter would be referred to the police authorities and also action will be initiated to terminate the services of Mr. A.

Mrs. X will be appraised of the action taken and will be requested to reconsider her resignation. In case however, the enquiry finds Mr. A not guilty, the resignation of Mrs. X will be accepted and the matter closed.

CASE 10

The Issue:

You are a no-nonsense, honest officer. You have been transferred to a remote district to head a department that is notorious for its inefficiency and callousness. You find that the main cause of the poor state of affairs is the indiscipline of a section of employees. They do not work themselves and also disrupt the working of others. You first warned the troublemakers to mend their ways or else face disciplinary action. When the warming had little effect, you issued a show cause notice to the ringleaders. As a retaliatory measures, these troublemakers instigated a woman employee amongst them to file a complaint of sexual harassment against you with the Women's Commission. The Commission promptly seeks your explanation. The matter is also publicized in the media to embarrass you further. Some of the options to handle this situation could be as follows:

(a) Give your explanation to the Commission and go soft on the disciplinary action.

(b) Ignore the Commission and proceed firmly with the disciplinary action.

(c) Brief your higher-ups, seek directions from them and act accordingly.

Recommended Approach

Each of the suggested options suffers from a serious defect.

(a) Going "soft" is a clear sign of the weakness. Having issued a warning and followed it up with a show cause notice to selected persons, it would be disastrous for the work ethic of the department not to pursue the matter to its logical conclusion. Such a retreat would only make matters much worse in a situation that is bad enough as it is.It would tantamount to throwing up one's hands in despair and abandoning all hope of improving the ambience within the department.

(b) Ignoring the notice of the Women's Commission, a statutory body, would be improper. It may even attract disciplinary action. In any case one would wish to cooperate sincerely in the discharge of legitimate functions by an important body.

(c) This would amount to abdicating one's legitimate responsibility. Passing the buck would be a sign of weakness and can only encourage the trouble makers and embarrass the superiors. Such a reaction is not expected from and effective leaders.

It would therefore the correct

- to proceed firmly with the disciplinary action already initiated
- apprise the Commission of the facts of the matter and
- keep the higher echelons informed of the developments as a measure of prudence as well as administrative propriety

Given the situation as described the very first step entailed the subsequent developments. There is no alternative but to press on with the course of action that one has set in motion. One must have faith and confidence that the system will protect you as you have acted in good faith, and support your effort to discipline those who are vitiating the atmosphere and resorting to blackmail.

References

- Anti Corruption Resource Centre. (n.d.). Overview of Corruption and Anticorruption Effort in India, *Transparency International.*

- Baumgartner R. (n.d.). Three Dimensions of Ethics, *Vocational Evaluation and Work Adjustment Bulletin/Winter.*

- Brovedani (2012) Emotional Intelligence and Business Ethics: The Necessary Factor for Transformational Leaders to Lead with Moral Principles

- Chouhan A.P.S. (2005). Good Governance in India by C. P. Barthwal, *the Indian Journal of Political Science,* Vol.66, No.3, pp 699-702.

- Constitution of India. (n.d.). In *Wikipedia.* Retrieved May 3, 2014, from http://en.wikipedia.org/wiki/Constitution_of_India

- Cooper, P. W. (n.d.). Final Understanding the "Key Issues and Constraints" in implementing the RTI Act. New Delhi.

- Dasgupta R. (2012). 11 Salient Features of the Constitution of India. Retrieved May 3, 2014, from http://www.preservearticles.com/201104235907/11-salient-features-of-the-constitution-of-india.html.

- Definitions and Types of Corruption. (2009). Retrieved April 6, 2014, from http://elaine.ie/2009/07/31/definitions-and-types-of-corruption/

- E-Governance and Good Governance: The Indian Context, *the Indian Journal of Political Science,* Vol.66, No.2, pp 313-32.

- Electoral Commission of Ghana. (n.d.). Retrieved 21 March, 2014, from http://img.modernghana.com/images/content/report_content/youthforgoodgovernance.pdf.

- Encyclopedia of Philosophy. (n.d.). Retrieved 2 March, 2014, from http://www.iep.utm.edu/ethics/

- Embezzlement. (n.d.). Retrieved May 1, 2014, from http://www.law.cornell.edu/wex/embezzlement.

- Evan M. Berman and Jonathan P. West: Emotional Intelligence in U.S. Cities: A Study of Social Skills among Public Managers (2012)

- Governance, C. F. Hand Book on Citizen Charter. Hyderabad: Centre for Good Governance.

- Governance, Y. F. Introduction to Corruption, World Bank.

- Harriss J. (2007). Antinomies of Empowerment: Observations on Civil Society, Politics and Urban Governance in India, *Economic and Political Weekly,* Vol.42, No.26, pp 2716-2724.

- Joseph and Newman (2010): Emotional Intelligence: An Integrative Meta-Analysis and Cascading Model (2009). Implementation of Right to Information Act:, New Delhi, *Observer Research Foundation.*

- Maesschalck (2003): Approaches to Ethics Management In The Public Sector

- Makrydemetres A. (n.d.). The 'ALIR' Imperatives of Ethical Reasoning, *Global Virtue Ethics Review*.
- Mukarji N. (1989). Changeful Society and Changeless Governance, *Economic and Political Weekly*, Vol.24, No.28, pp 1577+1579-1581.
- Nolan B. (1995). Committee on Standards in Public Life, London.
- Ombudsman. (n.d.). Retrieved January 2014, from http://www.ombudsman.gov.ua/en/index.php?option=com_content&view=article&id=1114&Itemid=22.
- Pelletier and Blig: 2006: Rebounding from Corruption: Perceptions of Ethics Program Effectiveness in a Public Sector Organization
- Rajya Sabha. (1997). Retrieved January 2014, from http://rajyasabha.nic.in/rsnew/publication_electronic/ethics_committee.pdf.
- Rajya Sabha. (n.d.). Retrieved April 1, 2014, from http://rajyasabha.nic.in/rsnew/rsat_work/chapter-9.pdf.
- Rajya Sabha. Code of Conduct for Members of Rajya Sabha. (n.d.). Retrieved May 3, 2014, from http://rajyasabha.nic.in/rsnew/members/code_conduct.pdf.
- Rao S.L. (2000). Competition, Ethics and Governance, *Economic and Political Weekly*, Vol. 35, No. 34, pp 3015-3019.

- Reddy S. R. (n.d.). Institutional Arrangements to Combating Corruption a Comparative Study India's (C.B.I) and Nalsar Law Review.
- Saxena A. (2005). Ombudsman Association, Retrieved 2014, from http://www.ombudsmanassociation.org/ (Cooper).
- Shankar M. (n.d.). Lokpal and Lokayukta in India, Academia.edu.
- Sims, and Brinkmann: 2002, Leaders as Moral Role Models: The Case of John Gutfreund at Salomon Brothers'
- Som L.S. (2006). Corporate Governance Codes in India. *Economic and Political Weekly*, Vol. 41, No. 39, pp 4153-4160.

About the Author

Dr. Mohan Kanda, a retired Indian Administrative Service officer of Andhra Pradesh Cadre has spent over four decades in public service and has served the state and the central governments in several capacities in various important departments, including as Secretary to the Government of India and Chief Secretary to the Government of Andhra Pradesh. He holds a Doctorate in Cooperative Agricultural Credit.

After retirement from the service, Dr. Kanda served as a Member of the National Disaster Management Authority (NDMA), Government of India, and as a Member of the Steering Committee of the Planning Commission for the formulation of the 12th Five Year Plan for "Agriculture and Allied Sectors".

Currently, Dr. Kanda is a Member of the Board of Supervision of the National Bank for Agriculture and Rural Development (NABARD); Visiting Faculty at the Centre for Atmospheric Studies, Indian Institute of Technology (IIT), New Delhi; Adjunct Faculty at the Indo-German Centre for Sustainability, Department of Humanities and Social Studies, Indian Institute of Technology (IIT), Chennai: Member of the Court, Central University, Rajasthan; and Member of the Board of Management of the Sri Sathya Sai Institute of Higher Learning, Andhra Pradesh.

Dr. Kanda has helped shape several national policies including the National Policy on Agriculture, the National Policy on Cooperatives and the National Policy on Rehabilitation and Resettlement of Project-Affected Persons. He has also contributed significantly to the formulation of the law governing Multi-State Cooperatives.

Earlier publications by Dr. Kanda include;

1. The Tinctured Canvas - Concept Practice & Strategies in Rural Development (Published by Bharatiya Vidya Bhavan, Mumbai)
2. Vasundhara - An Anthology of Land Resources in India (Published by the Council for Advancement of People's Action and Rural Technology [CAPART], Ministry of Rural Development, Government of India)
3. Forgiving Earth - The Dynamics of Policy Support Reforms for the Millennium Farmer in the Asia Pacific Region (Published by Catalyst Publications, New Delhi)
4. "Not by Others' Hands" - An Anthology of a Century of Credit Cooperatives in India (A tribute to the Cooperative Movement in the International Year of Cooperation 2012) - Published by Global Research Publications, New Delhi.
5. Mohana Makarandam, Telugu book based on his experiences as bureaucrat came as serial in Swathi, Telugu weekly magazine.

THE HANS INDIA
An English Daily

The Hans India *11 May, 2014*

Ethics in Governance (First Edition)

Book Release Function

The book was released on 10th May, 2014 at a function held at Centre for Good Governance (CGG) Hyderabad. The book is published by CGG and released by Justice B. Chandra Kumar of High Court of A.P. The event was presided by Shri K Ramakrishna Rao, IAS, Special Secretary Finance (IF) to the Govt. of Telangana and Director General, Centre for Good Governance. Shri M. Gopala Krishna, IAS (retd.) was the Guest of Honour for the event and introduced the book. Shri Devi Prasad Juvvadi, Director (Agriculture Management), CGG invited the guests and Dr.B.Gangaiah, ADG, CGG proposed vote of thanks.

NEED FOR RIGHT PERSONS MAKING HONEST DECISIONS

- *Justice Chandra Kumar lauds honest officers not buckling under pressure*
- *Releases book 'Ethics in Governance Resolution of Dilemmas' authored by retired IAS officer Mohan Kanda*

OUR BUREAU

(From left) Centre for Good Governance director general K Ramakrishna Rao, AP High Court Justice B Chandra Kumar, Retd IAS officer M Gopala Krishna and author Mohan Kanda releasing the book 'Ethics in Governance – Resolution of Dilemma' in Hyderabad on Sunday

Hyderabad: This was the time the 'intellectuals' and the 'honest resourceful persons' influence the society and take forward the country in the right direction, said Justice B Chandra Kumar of AP the High Court, while releasing the book 'Ethics in Governance – Resolution of Dilemmas', authored by retired IAS officer Mohan Kanda.

He applauded the sincerity of officers in civil services who stood strong on their values despite challenges, and emphasised the role played by them in making a better society.

According to the Judge, the honest officers and individuals try to find the 'truth' by their instinctive correct observation. Moreover, they use their own brains; they do not fall prey to prejudice and are 'close to truth'. He stressed that everyone should introspect and asked how many were close to truth.

Justice Chandra Kumar said there were various factors that influenced the decision-making at higher levels; therefore there was a need for right persons for making honest decisions. He held at high esteem the officers who did not buckle under administrative pressure and maintained their stature in testing times. Acknowledging the efforts put forward by former officials like Mohan Kanda, he hoped that all retired civil servants would look forward to contributing their experience and expertise to society.

Further, he stressed the role of parents and teachers in inculcating honest values and truthfulness in children, so that they grow up to responsible and honest citizens.

Retired IAS, M Gopala Krishna said the book 'Ethics in Governance' had been released at the right time, when India was facing corruption, crime, communalism and casteism. "These are the times when the greed is overtaking 'need' or 'want', and is affecting the civil servants," he said, adding only good people could ensure good governance.

Disclosing some of the facets of his book, Mohan Kanda said that as 'Ethics' was not a static subject he tried to focus on contemporary problems faced by the administration in the country. He said that the book was written with the perspective that people were the 'ultimate bosses'. K Ramakrishna Rao, Director-General, Centre for Good Governance, and retired IAS S Chakravarthy were among other speakers on the occasion.

ఆంధ్రజ్యోతి
మా అక్షరం మీ ఆయుధం 11 May, 2014

'ఎథిక్స్ ఇన్ గవర్నెన్స్' పుస్తకాన్ని ఆవిష్కరిస్తున్న హైకోర్టు జస్టిస్ చంద్రకుమార్, గోపాలకృష్ణ, రామకృష్ణారావు, మోహన్‌కందా

నిర్ణయాల్లో నిజాయతీ ముఖ్యం

1 **జస్టిస్ చంద్రకుమార్**

హైదరాబాద్, మే 11(ఆంధ్రజ్యోతి): మేధావులు తీసుకునే నిర్ణయాల్లో నిజాయతీ ఉంటేనే దేశానికి, సమాజానికి మేలు జరుగుతుందని హైకోర్టు న్యాయమూర్తి బి.చంద్ర కుమార్ అన్నారు. ప్రభుత్వంలోని కీలక అధికారులు తీసుకునే నిర్ణయాలు ప్రజల కష్టాలు, కన్నీళ్లు తొలగించేలా ఉండాలన్నారు. రాష్ట్ర ప్రభుత్వ మాజీ ప్రధాన కార్యదర్శి డాక్టర్ మోహన్‌కందా రచించిన 'ఎథిక్స్ ఇన్ గవర్నెన్స్' పుస్తకాన్ని హైదరాబాద్‌లో ఆది వారం ఆయన ఆవిష్కరించారు. ఈ సందర్భంగా జస్టిస్ చంద్రకుమార్ మాట్లాడుతూ దేశ భవిష్యత్తు మేధావుల ఆలోచనపైనే ఆధారపడి ఉంటుందన్నారు. 'మనం ఎవరికి సేవ చేయడానికి వచ్చాం, ఎవరికి చేస్తున్నాం' అనేది దృష్టిలో పెట్టుకొని నీతి, నిజాయి తీతో నిర్ణయాలు తీసుకోవాలని ఆకాంక్షించారు. నిర్ణయాలు తీసుకునేముందు అందులో దేశ శ్రేయస్సు ఉందా? సమాజానికి మేలు జరుగుతుందా? మంత్రికో, మనకో ఉపయో గకరమా? అనేది ఆలోచించాలని సూచించారు. కులం, మతం, ధనం, స్వార్థం అనే నాలుగింటిని దూరంగా ఉంచకపోతే దేశానికి చాలా ప్రమాదమని హెచ్చరించారు. వందల కోట్లు సంపాదించి పిల్లలకు ఇచ్చినా.. మనవళ్లు తాతా మాకేమిచ్చావని అడుగు తారని, అందర్నీ సంతృప్తి పరచడం సాధ్యం కాదన్నారు. సమాజం కోసం బతకాలను కునే ప్రతి ఒక్కరూ విసుగు, విరామం లేకుండా అవినీతికి వ్యతిరేకంగా పోరాడితేనే రేపటి తరానికి మహోన్నత భారతావనిని ఇవ్వగలమని తెలిపారు. అవినీతిని అరికట్టక పోతే రేపటి తరం రక్తహీనతతో చనిపోతుందని ఆందోళన వ్యక్తం చేశారు. పుస్తక రచ యిత మోహన్‌కందా మాట్లాడుతూ నైతిక విలువలు అందరికీ ఉంటాయని, వాటిని ఎప్పుడు ఎలా ఉపయోగించాలో ఓ పద్ధతి ప్రకారం కూర్పుచేసిందే తన పుస్తకమ న్నారు. రిటైర్డ్ ఐఏఎస్ అధికారి గోపాలక్రిష్ణ మాట్లాడుతూ నాలుగు 'సీ'లను (కరప్షన్, క్రైమ్, క్యాస్టిజమ్, కమ్యూనలిజం) దూరంగా ఉంచితేనే మేధావి అనేదానికి అర్థం ఉంటుందన్నారు. డాక్టర్ మర్రి చెన్నారెడ్డి హెచ్‌ఆర్‌డీ డైరెక్టర్ జనరల్ కె.రామకృష్ణారావు మాట్లాడుతూ పరిపాలనలో గవర్నెన్స్ చాలా కీలకమైందని, రాష్ట్రంలో ఈ గవర్నెన్స్‌ను మెరుగుపరచడానికి ఎంసీహెచ్‌ఆర్‌డీ కృషి చేస్తోందని చెప్పారు.

Release of Ethics in Governance, Telugu Translation - Paripaalanalo Dharmapalana

The Telugu translation of the book 'Ethics in Governance' 'Paripaalanalo Dharmapalana' authored by Dr. Mohan Kanda, I.A.S. (Retd.), former Chief Secretary to Government of AP, was released on 20th March, 2015. The book was published by Centre for Good Governance (CGG). Padma Bhushan Shri K Padmanabaiah, IAS (Retd.), Former Home Secretary, GoI attended as Chief Guest and released it at a function held at Centre for Good Governance, Hyderabad. The event was presided by Shri K Ramakrishna Rao, IAS, Special Secretary Finance (IF) to the Govt. of Telangana and Director General, CGG. Dr.Phani Kumar, IAS (Retd.) former Director General, CGG was the Guest of Honour for the event and introduced the book.

Shri Padmanabaiah observed that accountability and responsibility have to be brought in to ensure ethics in governance and that a support system is needed to protect upright officers in these days of declining ethics. Further, Shri Padmanabaiah felt that as the Union Public Service Commission (UPSC) has a separate paper of 300 marks on ethics, this book written by an experienced bureaucrat with practical insights will be of great help to students preparing for the competitive exams.

Former bureaucrat Shri Phani Kumar said there cannot be a better book on ethics in governance at a time when politicians are hopping from one party to the other in quest of power by setting aside all ideals. Shri Devi Prasad Juvvadi, Director (Agriculture Management), CGG invited the guests.

విలువలతోపాటు జవాబుదారీతనం ఉండాలి

బంజారాహిల్స్,మార్చి 20(నమస్తే తెలంగాణ): నిత్యజీవితంలో విలువలు పాటించడంతో పాటు చిత్తశుద్ధి,జవాబుదారీతనంతో వ్యవహరించాలని కేంద్ర హోంశాఖ మాజీ కార్యదర్శి కె.పద్మనాభయ్య అన్నారు. సెంటర్ ఫర్ గుడ్ గవర్నెన్స్, తెలంగాణ ప్రభుత్వం ఆధ్వర్యంలో జూబ్లీహిల్స్‌లోని మర్రి చెన్నారెడ్డి మానవ వనరుల అభివృద్ధి సంస్థ ఆధ్వర్యంలో పుస్తకావిష్కరణ కార్యక్రమాన్ని నిర్వహించారు. ఈ కార్యక్రమానికి అతిథిగా హాజరైై రాష్ట్ర ప్రభుత్వ మాజీ ముఖ్య కార్యదర్శి మోహన్ కందా రచించిన 'పరిపాలనలో ధర్మపాలన' పుస్తకావిష్కరించారు. అనంతరం మాట్లాడుతూ..పరిపాలన వ్యవహారాల్లో నైతిక విలువలు పాటించడం కత్తిమీద సాములాంటిదేన్నారు.తెలంగాణ రాష్ట్ర స్పెషల్ సెక్రటరీ కె.రామకృష్ణారావు మాట్లాడుతూ.. సివిల్ సర్వీసెస్‌కు రావాలనుకునే వారికి పుస్తకం ఎంతో ప్రయోజనకరంగా ఉంటుందన్నారు. పుస్తక రచయిత మోహన్‌కందా మట్లాడుతూ..

పుస్తకాన్ని ఆవిష్కరిస్తున్న అతిథులు

సమర్థత, ప్రభావశీలత, పారదర్శకత (sic: పా దుపు), తదితర లక్షణాలతో పాలన సాగించడంతో పాటు ప్రజల అంచనాలను అందుకునేలా పరిపాలన సాగించాలని సూచించారు. సెంటర్ ఫర్ గుడ్ గవర్నెన్స్ డైరెక్టర్ జే.దేవీప్రసాద్,అదనపు డైరెక్టర్ డాక్టర్ జి.బాగయ్య పాల్గొన్నారు.

www.ingramcontent.com/pod-product-compliance
Lightning Source LLC
Chambersburg PA
CBHW071244230926
51849CB00001B/224